RETAIN
-ABILITY

RETAINING
TALENT

IN A COMPLEX WORKPLACE

JEFF BELSKY AND TOM SHANDY

PERCHERON
PUBLISHING

Percheron Publishing
152 Wabash St., Pittsburgh, PA 15220
hello@percheronpublishing.com

Paperback ISBN: 978-1-965559-05-5
eBook: 978-1-965559-07-9

Cover and book design by Jess LaGreca, Mayfly book design

Library of Congress Catalog Number: 2025905081
First Printing: 2025

CONTENTS

DEDICATION

We thank our families for their support, the executive contributors to this book for their words of wisdom, and our readers for being open-minded and willing to change.

ABOUT THIS BOOK

Ready or not, the future arrives.

This book gives leaders at all levels and in all sectors strategies to successfully increase the retention of Generation Y and Z employees—who prove that the future indeed has landed. And has landed with enough force and energy to swamp any organization unwilling or unable to accept the adaptations required.

Employee retention has taken a front-row seat regarding most organizational challenges. Attracting qualified employees is one thing—but keeping them is another! The cost of losing employees in today's dynamic and competitive human resource environment has become enormous. Unfortunately, no one "magic pill" exists to increase the retention of employees. However, certain tested strategies promise to improve organizational retention.

In this book, we concentrate on three primary strategies to help increase the retention of Generation Y and Z employees. It doesn't matter the organization's industry sector; the strategies can quickly be implemented to realize immediate results. Additionally, this book relates to all levels of organizational leaders.

More than simply an executive leadership or human resource function, the employee retention crisis impacts the overall organization, making the strategies to improve employee retention responsibility of everyone in the organization.

FOREWORD

Heraclitus, an ancient Greek philosopher from the city of Ephesus, wrote, *"The only constant is change."* Well, that's certainly true in business. The world of work is changing rapidly. It's transforming not just what we do but how we do it, and that means a change in the knowledge and expertise the business requires to get the job done. It makes sense, then, to ask why hiring managers find it increasingly difficult to identify people with the right skills to fill the need? In fact, most employers struggle (2023 ManpowerGroup survey). What doesn't make sense, though, is that business leaders can't hold on to the people they have. According to a recent global survey, 93% of organizations worry about employee retention (2023 Workplace Learning Report, LinkedIn Learning). They should. Like customer churn, employee churn can be devastating to a business. So, what's the problem? With this rapid change in work comes a corresponding and often necessary change in the workplace, which directly and significantly impacts people.

I believe that too many leaders inside and outside of HR struggle to understand the evolving needs and growing demands of a multi-generational workforce. As a result, they're still trying to figure out what to do about it. Enter Retain-ability. Before I retired as head of my employer's enterprise analytics center of excellence, I had the privilege of leading a cross-functional team established to address employee retention and growth. We started with Heraclitus' fundamental truth and built a model to engage, enable, and empower our generationally diverse workforce.

We did one critical thing that this book's authors so astutely recommend: we dedicated significant time and energy to integrating leadership, culture, and empowerment to ensure our community felt valued, respected, and heard. The result became an evergreen model for ensuring our people would always be future-ready. The authors and their experienced contributors offer powerful perspectives and actionable insight on a critical issue touching organizations everywhere. They get to the point of the challenges and opportunities in leveraging employee retention. And the tips they offer work. My team used many of them.

That makes this book timely, relevant, and well done.

—Gregory P. Steffine
Retired Analytics Enablement Leader and Author

INTRODUCTION: NAVIGATING THE GENERATIONAL TIDES

In the complex tapestry of modern organizational dynamics, retaining employees presents a formidable obstacle for businesses of all sizes and industries. As we delve into the labyrinth of data sourced from various reputable outlets, a stark reality emerges: the numbers tell a compelling story of organizations' struggles and successes in retaining their valuable talent. From the exorbitant costs associated with turnover to the profound impact of employee engagement on organizational performance, these statistics offer invaluable insights into the intricate web of factors shaping the retention landscape.

As we embark on this exploration, we will confront the staggering statistics that underscore the urgency and importance of effective retention strategies while also uncovering the hidden opportunities for growth and innovation that lie within. Through the lens of data-driven analysis, we will illuminate the path forward in navigating the complex terrain of employee retention in today's organizations.

- 51% of currently employed workers say they are watching for or actively seeking a new job. (Gallup, 2023)

- The average tenure of an employee is 4.1 years. Workers aged 55 to 64 had an average tenure of 9.9 years, while workers aged 25 to 34 had an average tenure of only 2.8 years. (*Bureau of Labor Statistics, 2023*)

- 24% of Millennials think about finding new jobs within two years. (Deloitte, 2023)

- 38% of Millennials expect to stay fewer than five years with the same employer. (*Deloitte, 2023*)

- 60% of Millennials are open to different job opportunities. (*Gallup, 2023*)

- 54% of Generation Z will search for new jobs within a year. (*TechRepublic*)

- 30% of new hires leave within 90 days. The reasons employees leave isn't a shocker: 43% say the role doesn't meet their expectations, 34% leave because of a specific incident, and 32% don't think the company culture is a good fit. (*HBR, 2024*)

- Companies with a structured onboarding program keep 58% of employees for three years. Furthermore, 77% of new hires with official onboarding programs hit their first performance milestone. (*LinkedIn, 2024*)

- Nearly 38% of employees quit within the first year of employment. Over 40% of employees who leave within the first year do so in the first 90 days. Employees most often left during this time frame because of a lack of career development opportunities, job characteristics they didn't like, and poor work-life balance. (*Work Institute, 2024*)

RETAINING EMPLOYEES—
A NATIONAL PROBLEM

Retaining employees has become a pressing national problem affecting organizations across all sectors. In today's highly competitive job market, characterized by low unemployment rates and high demand for skilled workers, organizations face unprecedented challenges in retaining their talent. Several factors contribute to this widespread issue, ranging from shifting demographic trends to evolving employee expectations and workplace dynamics.

The changing demographics of the workforce represents a key factor in driving the retention crisis, particularly the aging of the baby boomer generation and the influx of younger generations such as Gen Y and Z. As baby boomers retire in large numbers, organizations grapple with a significant loss of institutional knowledge and experience. At the same time, younger generations bring different values, priorities, and expectations to the workplace, placing new demands on organizations to adapt their retention strategies accordingly.

The rise of the gig economy and the increasing prevalence of remote work also have reshaped the employment landscape, making it easier for employees to explore alternative job opportunities and switch employers more frequently. The proliferation of online job platforms and social media networks has made it easier for employees to connect with potential employers and explore new career opportunities, further fueling turnover rates.

Moreover, employee expectations have evolved significantly in recent years, with workers increasingly prioritizing factors such as work-life balance, career development opportunities, and positive work culture over traditional perks and benefits. Organizations that fail to meet these evolving expectations risk losing their top talent to competitors who offer more attractive work environments and growth opportunities.

The impact of high turnover rates extends beyond individual organizations, with broader implications for the economy. High turnover can disrupt business operations, lead to decreased productivity and morale, and increase recruitment and training costs for organizations. Furthermore, turnover can erode customer satisfaction and loyalty, as employees project the face of the organization and play a critical role in delivering quality products and services.

In response to these challenges, organizations must prioritize employee retention as a strategic imperative and invest in initiatives to attract, engage, and retain their talent. This may include offering competitive compensation and benefits packages, providing opportunities for professional development and advancement, fostering a supportive and inclusive work culture, and promoting work-life balance and flexibility. By addressing the root causes of turnover and implementing proactive retention strategies, organizations can mitigate the negative impact of employee churn and position themselves for long-term success in today's competitive business environment.

EMBARKING ON THE JOURNEY

In the ever-shifting seas of the modern workplace, one thing has become abundantly clear: the workforce is undergoing a seismic transformation, and the generations at its helm, Gen Y and Z, have charted a course unlike any before. The voyage of leading and retaining these generations has proved to be both exhilarating and challenging, akin to navigating uncharted waters, where the currents of technology, culture, and values converge in a complex mosaic.

In this prologue, we embark on a journey to understand the profound intricacies of retaining Gen Y and Z employees—a journey through the very heart of a complex and ever-evolving landscape, where the traditional rules of engagement no longer suffice and where the captaining of a multigenerational crew requires nimbleness, adaptability, and a keen eye for what sets these generations apart.

THE RISE OF THE DIGITAL NATIVES:

Imagine a generation born into a world that had already digitized its foundations—the generation known as Gen Z. They grew up with smartphones as extensions of their hands, seamlessly navigating virtual realms as naturally as they did the physical. Millennials, or Gen Y, pioneers of the digital revolution, witnessed the transition from analog to digital and adapted along the way. For both, technology isn't merely a tool; it's the very essence of how they connect, work, and live. To lead and retain such digital natives requires not just an understanding but a fluency in the ever-evolving tech landscape.

SHAPING VALUES AMID COMPLEXITY:

As we delve into the generational intricacies, we encounter a tapestry of values and beliefs that shape the sails of Gen Y and Gen Z. These generations share a profound desire for meaningful work, a commitment to innovation, and an insistence on transparency. Yet, they unfurl their individual flags, each bearing its unique emblem—Gen Y, valuing experience and work-life balance, and Gen Z, emphasizing financial security and adaptability. These shared values and distinctive priorities create a dynamic where leadership must be versatile and responsive, attuned to the shifting winds of generational expectations.

THE CULTURAL NEXUS:

As we embark on this journey through the uncharted waters of retaining Gen Y and Z in today's complex world, we find that the challenges yield boundless opportunities. The talent, innovation, and energy of these groups have the potential to propel organizations to new horizons. This book serves as our compass, guiding us through the intricacies of leading and retaining these generations while helping us uncover the treasures that lie beneath the surface of this generational sea.

The following chapters explore the strategies, insights, and practical approaches empowering leaders and organizations to thrive in this dynamic era, ensuring that they not only navigate these generational tides but harness their full potential for success.

Retaining talent represents one of the most important initiatives organizations face in today's dynamic and ever-changing environment. Human resource professionals must seek every avenue to improve employee retention. Frustration ramps high. Organizations that improve employee retention can emerge more powerful than ever.

ABOUT THE EXECUTIVE CONTRIBUTORS

The executive contributors to this book represent invaluable assets, bringing a wealth of expertise and experience from diverse industry sectors to the table. Their insights and perspectives provide a comprehensive understanding of the challenges and opportunities surrounding employee retention in today's complex business landscape.

With their deep knowledge of organizational dynamics, human resources strategies, and leadership principles, these executives offer invaluable insights that shed light on the multifaceted nature of employee retention and its implications for organizational success. Their expert opinions not only enrich the content of this book but also offer practical guidance and actionable strategies for navigating the complexities of talent management and fostering a culture of retention and engagement within organizations.

As leaders in their respective fields, their contributions serve as a testament to the importance of collaboration and knowledge-sharing in addressing the critical issues facing businesses today.

We would like to thank these individuals for their expert contributions.

Hannah Godfrey
Performance Review Institute, London, England
Vice President, Professional Development

Mickey Herbert, DBA
Gallagher
Branch President and Executive Vice President of Marketing

Jonathan Hicks
Philips
Director of Program Management

Jason Morwick
MacRae Business Solutions, Inc.
Chief Executive Officer & President

Navin Parmar, BE (Hons), MBA
Co-Founder and Vice President, Interlink Analytics, Inc.
Senior Data and AI Executive, Microsoft Inc.

Jeanine Selover
ITS
Vice President of Organizational Development

Nate Smith
Alliant Insurance Services
First Vice President, Data Security

Alexandra Wisenall, DNP, MBA, APRN, FNP-BC
WVU Medicine, East
Assistant Vice President, Ambulatory Operations of System
    Medical Group

CHAPTER 1

DEFINING THE RETENTION CHALLENGE

THE COST OF NOT RETAINING EMPLOYEES

The cost of not retaining employees can be substantial, encompassing both direct financial expenses and broader organizational challenges.

According to SHRM (Society for Human Resource Management), the cost of losing an employee can amount to double that employee's annual salary—depending on the role and level of experience. And while that may sound extreme, it becomes entirely plausible once broken down into chunks. Think about what it takes to bring on a new employee. Think about the last time you started a job—what did it take for you to really get up to speed? Depending on the job, the upfront costs associated with onboarding a new employee can be staggering. Losing that same employee—especially a high performer—can be more than realized when you look at all the individual components.

DEFINING EMPLOYEE TURNOVER COSTS

The cost of an employee leaving a company, often referred to as "employee turnover cost," can vary widely depending on several factors, including the employee's role, the industry, the organization's size, and the reason for departure. Some key cost components associated with employee turnover include:

RECRUITMENT AND HIRING COSTS:

Recruiting and hiring new employees incur various costs and implications for organizations, both tangible and intangible. Tangible costs include expenses associated with advertising job openings, conducting interviews, and processing paperwork. Additional costs relate to background checks, drug screenings, and pre-employment assessments. Beyond these direct expenditures, indirect costs cover time spent by HR personnel and hiring managers in the recruitment process, and productivity losses during the transition period when positions remain vacant. Moreover, hiring the wrong candidate can result in costly turnover, wasted training investments, and drops in productivity. Furthermore, intangible costs also impact team morale and organizational culture when a new hire does not fit well within the team dynamics or fails to meet expectations. Therefore, understanding the full spectrum of costs associated with recruitment and hiring remains crucial for organizations to make informed decisions and optimize their talent acquisition strategies.

Advertising job openings

Advertising for job openings incurs various organizational costs, significantly impacting recruitment budgets. These costs can range from traditional print advertisements in newspapers and industry publications to digital platforms such as job boards, social media, and professional networking sites. Print advertising expenses typically include design fees, printing costs, and placement fees based on the size and prominence of the ad. On the other hand, digital advertising often involves pay-per-click or pay-per-impression models, where companies pay based on the number of clicks or views their ads receive. Additionally, costs may be associated with sponsored job postings on online job boards or social media platforms to increase visibility and reach targeted candidates. Companies may invest in SEO (search engine optimization) techniques to ensure their job postings appear prominently in search engine results, driving organic traffic to their career pages. Understanding the diverse advertising options and associated costs is essential for organizations to effectively allocate resources and attract qualified candidates to their job openings.

Recruiter or staffing agency fees

Utilizing a recruiter or staffing agency to hire new employees can entail significant costs for organizations. Still, it offers distinct advantages in terms of efficiency and access to a broader talent pool. These costs typically involve fees paid to the recruiting agency, which can be structured in various ways, including contingency fees based on successful placements or retained fees for exclusive recruitment services. Contingency fees get calculated as a percentage of the hired candidate's first-year salary, paid upon successful placement. Retained fees, on the other hand, involve an upfront payment to secure the services of the recruiting agency exclusively for a particular search. Additional costs may be associated with background checks, drug screenings, and other pre-employment assessments, depending on the services provided by the agency. Despite these costs, many companies opt to work with recruiters or staffing agencies to streamline the hiring process, tap into specialized expertise, and access passive candidates who may not be actively seeking employment.

Screening and interviewing candidates

Screening and interviewing candidates to hire new employees can incur significant costs for organizations in terms of time and resources. These costs encompass various activities, including resume screening, initial phone screenings, in-person interviews, background checks, and reference checks. Each stage of the screening and interviewing process requires allocation of staff time, from HR personnel reviewing resumes to hiring managers conducting interviews. There also may be expenses associated with conducting background checks through third-party providers and verifying candidate references. Companies often use methods to screen and interview candidates efficiently, such as applicant tracking systems (ATS) to manage resumes, video interviews to assess remote candidates, and behavioral assessments to evaluate soft skills. Some organizations also utilize panel interviews or structured interview techniques to ensure consistency and fairness in the evaluation process.

Skills assessment and testing
Requiring skills assessments and testing as part of the hiring process, while incurring various costs for organizations, remain instrumental in ensuring that candidates possess the necessary competencies for the job. These costs include developing or procuring assessment tools, administering tests, and evaluating results. Companies may invest in specialized software or platforms for skills testing, which often involve licensing fees or subscription costs. Other personnel costs include administering tests, proctoring exams, and scoring assessments. Companies may incur expenses for training staff members to interpret test results accurately and make informed hiring decisions based on assessment outcomes. Examples of skills assessment methods include technical proficiency tests, situational judgment tests, personality assessments, and cognitive ability tests. Some companies also incorporate practical exercises or simulations to evaluate candidates' skills in real-world scenarios.

Background checks and reference checks
Conducting background checks and reference checks as part of the hiring process generates expenses for organi-

zations, but represent a crucial step in mitigating risks associated with potential hires. These costs encompass fees associated with outsourcing background check services to third-party providers, which may be charged based on the depth and scope of the checks required. Background checks typically include criminal history searches, verification of employment history, education verification, and checking for any professional licenses or certifications. Companies may also incur costs related to contacting and verifying references provided by candidates, which involves allocating staff time to conduct interviews and gather feedback. Some organizations opt to use online platforms or software solutions to streamline the background check process and automate certain tasks, reducing administrative overheads.

ONBOARDING AND TRAINING COSTS:

Onboarding and training new employees create costs for organizations, encompassing both direct expenses and indirect impacts on productivity and resources. Direct costs include expenses related to developing training materials, conducting training sessions, and providing necessary equipment or materials for new hires. Additional costs include dedicating staff time to onboarding activities like mentorship, shadowing, and supervision, as well as external training programs, workshops, or seminars designed to enhance employees' skills and knowledge. Indirect costs stem from lost time and productivity as new hires acclimate to their roles and become fully productive team members. These costs can include decreased efficiency, errors or mistakes during the learning curve, and potential disruptions to workflow. Investing in onboarding and training remains essential for nurturing talent and fostering employee development, just as understanding and managing the associated costs related to optimizing organizational resources and achieving long-term success.

Orientation and training programs

New hire orientation and training represent critical investments for organizations, as they facilitate the smooth integration of new employees into the company culture and equip them with the necessary skills and knowledge to perform their roles effectively. The costs associated with orientation and training encompass various elements, including developing orientation materials, allocating staff time for conducting sessions, and providing training resources and facilities. Companies may incur expenses for hiring external trainers or facilitators, especially for specialized training programs or workshops. More indirect costs come with a temporary decrease in productivity, as new hires undergo orientation and training, structured orientation sessions covering company policies, culture, and values, as well as on-the-job training, mentorship programs, and e-learning modules tailored to specific job roles. Some organizations also leverage technology, like LMS (learning management systems), VR (virtual reality), or AR (augmented reality), to deliver engaging and interactive training experiences.

Provision of equipment, tools, and uniforms

Providing new employees with equipment, tools, and uniforms incurs tangible costs for organizations, as they must invest in acquiring and maintaining these resources to support employees in their roles. The costs of providing equipment and tools include purchasing or leasing expenses, plus ongoing maintenance and repair costs to ensure their functionality and safety. Additional expenses may relate to customizing equipment or tools to meet the specific needs of individual employees or job roles. Similarly, outfitting employees with uniforms entails costs such as purchasing uniforms, embroidering company logos or employee names, and laundering services.

Time and salaries spent by trainers and mentors
Employing trainers and mentors for new employees incurs significant costs for organizations, encompassing salaries or consulting fees paid to experienced professionals imparting knowledge and skills to new hires. Additional expenses may relate to training materials, resources, and facilities used by trainers and mentors to deliver effective instruction and guidance. Companies may also invest in training and certification programs to qualify internal employees as trainers or mentors.

PRODUCTIVITY LOSS:

The departure of employees from an organization can significantly impact productivity, stemming from various factors that disrupt workflow and create gaps in knowledge and expertise. First is the immediate loss of output as departing employees transition out of their roles, requiring time for knowledge transfer and task reallocation. This transition period often leads to decreased efficiency and delays in project timelines, as remaining employees adjust to new responsibilities or cover for vacant positions. Moreover, the departure of experienced employees may result in a temporary decline in quality as their expertise and institutional knowledge can no longer be readily accessed. Indirect productivity losses associated with the recruitment and onboarding process for replacing departing employees may accumulate, including time and resources invested in sourcing candidates, conducting interviews, and providing training. Employee turnover can have intangible impacts on team morale and organizational culture, leading to decreased engagement and increased turnover among remaining staff. Overall, the loss of productivity resulting from employee departures underscores the importance of effective retention strategies and succession planning to minimize disruptions and maintain organizational performance.

Decreased productivity during the notice period

During the notice period when employees leave the organization, a notable decrease in productivity can significantly impact overall organizational performance. This period, typically ranging from two weeks to several months, presents challenges as departing employees often begin to disengage from their roles, focusing on their impending departure rather than their current responsibilities. As a result, tasks may remain incomplete, projects may stall, and deadlines may be missed. Moreover, the departure of key employees during this time can disrupt team dynamics and create uncertainty among the remaining staff, leading to decreased morale and motivation. Additionally, the need for departing employees to train their replacements or hand over their duties can further divert time and resources away from ongoing projects, exacerbating productivity losses. Overall, the decreased productivity during the notice period underscores the importance of effective succession planning and knowledge transfer strategies to mitigate disruptions and maintain organizational continuity.

The learning curve for the replacement employee

When employees leave an organization, the learning curve associated with their replacements presents significant implications, costs, and challenges. New employees stepping into vacant roles often encounter a steep learning curve as they familiarize themselves with the organization's responsibilities, processes, and culture. This learning curve can decrease productivity and efficiency during the transition period, as new hires require time to gain proficiency in their roles and become fully integrated team members. Costs associated with training and onboarding replacement employees, including allocating staff time, resources, and potentially external training programs, can rack up, along with turnover-induced learning curves disrupting workflow continuity, leading to delays in project timelines and potential setbacks in achieving organizational goals. The departure of experienced employees also may result in losing specialized knowledge and expertise, further exacerbating the learning curve for replacements. Overall, the learning curve implications associated with employee turnover underscore the importance of effective succession planning, knowledge transfer strategies, and ongoing support for new hires to minimize disruptions and facilitate smooth organizational transitions.

Disruption to team dynamics and workflow
When key employees depart from an organization, team dynamics and workflow disruption can be profound and far-reaching. Key employees often play critical roles within their teams, possessing specialized knowledge, skills, and experience integral to the smooth functioning of projects and processes. Their departure can create gaps in expertise and leadership, leading to uncertainty and instability within the team. Moreover, key employees often serve as mentors or informal leaders, guiding and supporting their colleagues, whose morale and motivation may suffer in their absence. Additionally, the departure of key employees can disrupt workflow continuity, as projects may be delayed or stalled while remaining team members adjust

to new roles or responsibilities. This disruption can lead to decreased productivity, missed deadlines, and potential setbacks in achieving organizational goals. Furthermore, the loss of key employees may erode trust and cohesion within the team as remaining members grapple with feelings of uncertainty and insecurity about the future direction of their work. Overall, the departure of key employees can have significant implications for team dynamics and organizational workflow, highlighting the importance of effective succession planning and strategies for mitigating the impact of turnover.

KNOWLEDGE AND EXPERTISE LOSS:

Knowledge and expertise represent invaluable assets that drive organizational success and sustainability. When employees leave, they take with them a wealth of knowledge, insights, and experience accumulated over years of service. This loss of knowledge can have profound and far-reaching implications for organizations, extending beyond just the departure of an individual employee.

One of the most significant costs of losing knowledge and expertise arrives in the disruption to project continuity and deadlines. When key employees depart, they often leave behind unfinished projects or tasks, leading to delays, setbacks, and missed deadlines. This can have cascading effects on other projects and initiatives, creating a domino effect of delays and inefficiencies that impact overall productivity and performance.

Moreover, the loss of knowledge and expertise can harm client relationships. Employees who have built a strong rapport and trust with clients over time possess valuable insights into client preferences, expectations, and needs. When these employees leave, it can disrupt existing client relationships, leading to dissatisfaction, mistrust, and even loss of business. This can have lasting repercussions on the organization's reputation, credibility, and revenue stream.

Furthermore, the loss of knowledge and expertise represents a depletion of institutional memory and experience within the organization. Employees who have been with the organization for an extended period possess valuable insights into its history, culture, and operations. This institutional knowledge establishes a foundation for decision-making, problem-solving, and strategic planning. When these employees leave, it can create gaps in organizational memory, hindering the organization's ability to learn from past experiences and avoid repeating mistakes.

Losing knowledge and expertise can have competitive implications for organizations, as well. In today's knowledge-driven economy, organizations must continuously innovate and adapt to stay ahead of the competition. Employees who possess specialized skills, industry knowledge, and innovative ideas represent essential assets in this regard. When these employees leave, it can put the organization at a competitive disadvantage, as competitors may capitalize on the knowledge gap to gain market share, attract talent, or develop new products and services.

The cost of losing knowledge and expertise extends far beyond just the departure of individual employees. It impacts project continuity and deadlines, client relationships, institutional memory, and competitive positioning. Therefore, organizations must prioritize employee retention efforts to preserve knowledge, maintain continuity, and sustain long-term success in today's competitive business landscape.

REMAINING EMPLOYEES MAY EXPERIENCE DECREASED MORALE AND ENGAGEMENT

Employee turnover can profoundly affect workforce morale, engagement, and overall dynamics. When employees leave, especially valued or long-tenured team members, it can create a ripple effect that reverberates throughout the organization, impacting the remaining employees' psychological well-being and job satisfaction.

Decreased morale and engagement among the remaining workforces rank among the most significant consequences of employee turnover. When employees witness their colleagues leaving, it can create feelings of uncertainty, anxiety, and disillusionment. This sense of instability can erode trust in leadership, diminish confidence in the organization's stability, and lead to a loss of motivation and commitment among remaining employees. Increased stress from workload assignments and taking on the tasks of departed employees can exacerbate feelings of burnout among remaining employees. With fewer resources and manpower available to handle the workload, employees may be stretched thin, struggling to meet deadlines and deliverables. This can increase stress, fatigue, and job dissatisfaction, further impacting morale and engagement levels.

The impact of employee turnover on team cohesion cannot be understated. When key team members depart, it can disrupt established working relationships, communication channels, and collaboration efforts. The remaining team members may feel a sense of loss or disconnection, making it challenging to maintain productivity and cohesiveness. This can result in decreased teamwork, coordination, and synergy, ultimately impacting the organization's ability to achieve its goals and objectives. The work-life balance for remaining employees can be significantly impacted by increased stress and overwork resulting from employee turnover. With heavier workloads and fewer resources available, employees may struggle to balance their professional responsibilities and personal lives. This can lead to feelings of resentment, exhaustion, and dissatisfaction, further contributing to decreased morale and engagement levels.

Overall, the impact of employee turnover extends beyond just the departure of individual employees. It can profoundly affect the entire organization's morale, engagement, and team dynamics. By recognizing the potential consequences of turnover on employee well-being and organizational culture, organizations can take proactive steps to mitigate its negative effects. This includes investing in employee support programs, fostering open communication and transparency, and prioritizing employee retention efforts to preserve morale, engagement, and team cohesion in the face of turnover challenges.

POSSIBLE NEGATIVE EFFECTS ON CUSTOMER SERVICE

Employee turnover can have far-reaching consequences beyond just an organization's internal operations—it can also significantly impact current customer relationships and erode trust in the organization's brand. When employees leave, especially those with client-facing roles or strong relationships with customers, it can create uncertainty and concern among clients, leading to questions about the organization's stability and reliability.

One of the most significant impacts of employee turnover on customer relationships is the potential for clients to question the organization's ability to retain talent. When a valued employee departs, especially if instrumental in managing client accounts or providing personalized service, clients may wonder why the employee chose to leave and what it says about the organization's culture and leadership. This can lead to doubts about the organization's commitment to customer satisfaction and long-term partnerships. Departing employees may exacerbate the situation by bad-mouthing the organization in front of clients or fabricating negative information about product quality, company culture, or service standards. This can damage the organization's reputation and credibility, especially if the allegations are made to clients who have established trust and loyalty with the departing employee. Restoring client trust and confidence in the organization's integrity can be costly and time-consuming, requiring transparent communication, consistent service delivery, and proactive relationship management.

Furthermore, when employees leave, they may take clients with them if they move to a competitive organization in the same industry. This can result in a loss of revenue and market share for the organization and further erosion of trust among remaining clients, who may question the organization's ability to retain key accounts and maintain a competitive advantage. Retaining or regaining client trust becomes paramount in such situations, requiring proactive efforts to demonstrate value, address concerns, and rebuild relationships. The new employee tasked with taking over the accounts of departed employees faces the challenge of living up to the relationships built by their predecessors. Clients may have established expectations and preferences based on their previous interactions with the departing employee, making it challenging for the new employee to establish credibility and rapport. This transition period can be fraught with uncertainty and potential pitfalls, requiring careful navigation and proactive relationship-building efforts to ensure a smooth transition and maintain client satisfaction.

The impact of employee turnover on customer relationships and trust cannot be underestimated. From questioning the organization's stability to potential damage to the brand reputation, the consequences of turnover extend beyond just internal operations. By prioritizing employee retention efforts and proactive client relationship management strategies, organizations can mitigate the negative impacts of turnover and preserve trust, loyalty, and satisfaction among their client bases.

DOLLARS AND CENTS

The cost of losing an employee can vary widely depending on various factors, including the industry, the employee's position, the organization's size, and geographic location. However, estimates suggest that the average cost of employee turnover can be significant. Approximate figures related to the employee skill level include:

Low-Skilled Positions: For lower-skilled or entry-level positions, turnover costs may be relatively lower, ranging from 30% to 50% of the employee's annual salary. This includes recruitment, hiring, and training expenses.

Mid-Level Positions: For mid-level positions, the cost of turnover can be more substantial, typically amounting to 100% to 150% of the employee's annual salary, attributable to the higher cost of finding and training replacement employees.

Highly Skilled or Executive Positions: For specialized roles or executive positions, turnover costs can be the most significant, often exceeding 200% of the employee's annual salary. Replacing senior talent involves extensive recruitment, onboarding, and transition expenses.

Conducting a thorough analysis that considers the unique circumstances and expenses associated with your recruitment and retention efforts becomes essential to determine the exact cost of losing an employee within your organization. This analysis should include recruitment costs, training expenses, lost productivity, and any other relevant factors. By understanding the true cost of employee turnover, organizations can make more informed decisions about their retention strategies and investments in talent management.

WHAT IS QUIET QUITTING?

"Quiet quitting," also known as "silent resignation" or "disengaged quitting," refers to a situation where an employee mentally checks out from their job without resigning. In other words, they disengage from their work, become less productive, and may even become apathetic toward their job and the organization.

Many reasons explain why employees become disengaged in their work. Later in this book, we will discuss some reasons why employees become disengaged and the responsibility of the manager to look out for early warning signs.

Some common signs and characteristics of quiet quitting include:

1. Decreased Productivity: Quietly quitting employees may start to produce lower-quality work, miss deadlines, or become less efficient in their tasks.

2. Reduced Initiative: They may stop taking the initiative to propose new ideas, offer suggestions for improvement, or participate actively in meetings and discussions.

3. Increased Absenteeism: Quiet quitters may start taking more sick days, vacation days, or personal leave to distance themselves from the workplace.

4. Lack of Enthusiasm: These employees exhibit a lack of energy and passion for their job. They no longer seem excited about their work or the organization's goals.

5. Limited Interaction: Quiet quitters may withdraw from workplace social interactions, contributing less to team dynamics and maintaining minimal communication with colleagues.

6. Resistance to Change: These employees may resist changes or new organizational initiatives, further contributing to a stagnant work environment.

7. Minimal Career Development: Employees quietly quitting often stop seeking opportunities for skill development, advancement, or additional responsibilities.

8. Mental and Emotional Detachment: A mental and emotional detachment from the job occurs with employees feeling disconnected from the organization's mission and values.

9. Looking for Other Opportunities: Quiet quitters may explore other job opportunities discreetly, such as updating their resumes or networking with other professionals.

10. Longer-Term Disengagement: This disengagement can persist over an extended period, sometimes even years, as employees remain in their roles without actively contributing.

Quiet quitting creates problems for organizations because it can lead to decreased productivity, lowered morale among other employees, and a negative impact on the workplace culture. Additionally, it can be challenging for employers to identify and address this issue, as employees may not openly express their dissatisfaction or intentions to leave.

To mitigate quiet quitting, organizations should prioritize employee engagement and create an environment where employees feel valued, motivated, and connected to their work. Regular feedback, opportunities for growth, recognition of contributions, and an open channel for addressing concerns represent essential elements in retaining and re-engaging disengaged employees.

Gen Y and Z are not immune to the phenomenon of quiet quitting, which can affect employees of all age groups. However, some specific reasons and dynamics may make members of these generations more prone to silent resignation:

1. **High Expectations and Idealism:**
   › Gen Y and Z often enter the workforce with high career expectations. They seek meaningful work, opportunities for personal growth, and alignment with their values. They may quietly disengage when they perceive a disconnect between their expectations and the reality of their job or workplace.

2. **Pursuit of Passion and Purpose:**
   › These generations more likely prioritize passion and purpose in their work. They may mentally check out when they feel their job lacks a sense of purpose or they're not making a meaningful impact.

3. **Desire for Continuous Learning:**
   › Gen Y and Z value opportunities for learning and development. They may disengage if they feel their job no longer offers these opportunities or that they've reached a plateau.

4. **Recognition and Feedback:**
   › Younger generations desire frequent feedback and recognition for their contributions. They may become disheartened if they perceive a lack of appreciation or feel that their work goes unnoticed.

5. **Flexibility and Autonomy:**
   › Gen Y and Z appreciate workplace flexibility and autonomy in managing tasks and schedules. When organizations impose rigid rules and micromanage their work, it can lead to disengagement.

6. **Technology and Remote Work:**
   › Gen Y and Z are digital natives comfortable with technology. The shift to remote work due to technological advancements during the COVID-19 pandemic has made it easier for them to quietly disengage while working remotely.

7. **Job Market Opportunities:**
   › The job market has evolved, making it easier for younger generations to explore other job opportunities online, even while employed. They may engage in discreet job searching and networking, increasing the chances of finding a new job without their current employer's knowledge.

8. **Entrepreneurial Aspirations:**
   › Many Gen Y and Z individuals have entrepreneurial aspirations. They may use their current job as a stepping stone to gain experience and skills while quietly planning their own ventures.

9. **Mental Health Considerations:**
   › Younger generations are more open about mental health and well-being. If they experience work-related stress, burnout, or mental health challenges and feel their employer is not supportive, they may choose to silently disengage as a coping mechanism.

10. **Changing Priorities**
    > Personal life and work-life balance remain
      paramount to these generations. If work demands
      encroach on personal time or priorities, they may
      mentally withdraw to protect their life outside
      of work.

Organizations should recognize the signs of quiet quitting among Gen Y and Gen Z employees and take proactive steps to address their concerns. This may involve providing opportunities for career development, feedback, recognition, and flexibility, as well as fostering a workplace culture that aligns with the values and expectations of these generations. Open communication channels and addressing potential sources of disengagement can help retain and re-engage employees who might otherwise silently resign.

SUMMARY OF CHAPTER 1: DEFINING THE RETENTION CHALLENGE

The first chapter of the book explores the profound and multi-faceted costs associated with employee turnover, emphasizing its financial, cultural, and operational implications. Drawing on insights from industry research, such as those by SHRM, the chapter explains that losing an employee can cost up to twice their annual salary, particularly for highly skilled roles. These costs encompass recruitment, onboarding, training, and productivity losses, alongside more intangible effects, such as disrupted team dynamics and diminished morale.

Employee turnover costs include tangible expenses like advertising job openings, recruiter fees, and candidate assessments, as well as indirect losses, such as decreased efficiency during notice periods, learning curves for new hires, and workflow disruptions. The chapter highlights the ripple effects on team cohesion, employee engagement, and organizational culture, all of which can lead to further turnover.

The narrative underscores the importance of knowledge retention, with departing employees often taking invaluable expertise and client relationships with them, potentially harming the organization's competitiveness and reputation. It also delves into the phenomenon of "quiet quitting," where employees disengage without formally resigning, leading to reduced productivity and workplace morale.

The chapter concludes by advocating for proactive retention strategies, emphasizing the need for organizations to invest in employee engagement, development, and leadership to mitigate the adverse effects of turnover. Recognizing the unique dynamics of younger generations, such as Gen Y and Z, the chapter offers insights into fostering workplace environments that align with their values, enhancing retention and organizational resilience.

KEY BULLET POINTS

- **Financial Impact:** Employee turnover costs can range from 30% to more than 200% of an employee's annual salary, depending on the role and organization.
- **Recruitment Expenses:** Includes advertising, recruiter fees, assessments, and candidate background checks.
- **Onboarding Costs:** Developing orientation programs, providing equipment, and offering training for new hires, all add substantial expenses.
- **Productivity Losses:** Departures cause delays, disrupt workflows, and decrease efficiency during transition periods.
- **Cultural Effects:** Turnover impacts morale, team dynamics, and organizational cohesion, leading to disengagement among remaining employees.
- **Knowledge Loss:** Departing employees take institutional memory, client relationships, and hard-won expertise, weakening competitive positioning.
- **Quiet Quitting:** Employees mentally disengage while remaining in their roles, leading to productivity and cultural challenges.
- **Generational Considerations:** Gen Y and Z prioritize growth, feedback, and work-life balance, necessitating tailored retention strategies.

KEY SKILLS AND APPROACHES

- **Leadership Development:** Cultivate visionary and supportive leaders who actively engage and inspire teams.
- **Retention Strategies:** Implement proactive measures, such as employee recognition, professional development programs, and competitive compensation.
- **Succession Planning:** Ensure knowledge transfer and readiness for transitions to minimize disruptions.
- **Workplace Culture:** Foster an inclusive and collaborative environment that aligns with employee values.
- **Feedback Mechanisms:** Provide regular, constructive feedback and recognition to enhance employee engagement.
- **Employee Well-Being:** Address mental health and work-life balance concerns to reduce burnout and disengagement.

QUESTIONS FOR DEEPER UNDERSTANDING

1. What financial and intangible costs has your organization experienced from employee turnover?
2. How does your organization ensure new hires quickly adapt and integrate into their roles?
3. What measures are in place to identify and address signs of disengagement, such as quiet quitting?
4. How does your workplace culture impact employee retention and overall satisfaction?
5. What strategies have been most effective in retaining high-performing employees in your experience?
6. How do you balance organizational goals with employee needs, particularly for younger generations like Gen Y and Z?

7. In what ways can knowledge transfer and succession planning mitigate the effects of employee departures?
8. How can organizations proactively strengthen client relationships to withstand the impacts of employee turnover?

CHAPTER 2

UNDERSTANDING THE GENERATIONS

Jonathan Hicks
Philips, Director PMO
TOPIC: How to Retain the Generation Y and Z Employees

As a director at Philips, I had a team of 12 Gen Y and Gen Zers scattered worldwide. I had numerous cultural challenges that varied by region. But one universal challenge on a global scale remained—the need for psychological safety.

In times past, a corporation stood as a steadier institution providing a certain modicum of security and safety. In contrast, the corporate world of today moves fast. The stability once enjoyed, now long gone, has been replaced with a high-anxiety, technology-enabled, rapid pace.

With the constant shifting, my team needed to know they could speak their mind freely, be heard, and put their passion to full use. As the manager, my success also hinged on that transparency—because I needed to understand when there was an issue on their teams or projects requiring my support.

I found the fastest path to building psychological safety on my team came through focusing on building trust between manager and employee. Establishing trust created a strong connection that served as an anchor amid the constant state of change around them. I provided the team vision; in return, they could focus their energy on the things that mattered. I provided transparency about my shortcomings, and they felt safe to share elements not working well on their team.

In all the aspects of creating safety, I felt one area resonated deeply across the globe and cultures—supporting the individual when dealing with personal matters. What is a personal matter? A back injury that required lying flat most hours of the day, a daughter who had a mysterious illness that pulled her out of school for six months, and a dying mother in the next room who needed constant care.

In the short term, these examples distracted my team members from their work and impacted their performance. But how I handled them as a manager created the difference between them checking out or leaning in.

These personal matters create strong, often embarrassing, emotions for the employee. However, handling them with grace as the manager creates a long-term momentum that greatly outweighs the short-term dip in job performance. What does grace look like? It doesn't mean ignoring or excusing their dip in performance. It's employing empathy to understand their situation. It's letting them know it's okay that their performance dips for a period (most employees feel some amount of guilt or shame about "dropping the ball" or letting others down, so address it). It's giving them the space, time, and resources they need to resolve the issue, and it's checking in with them along the way to see how things are going and recalibrate the plan.

A few things happen through this process. First, the employee finds relief, knowing he or she can fully address the personal issue. But secondly, as psychological safety arrives, that they become hard-pressed to walk away from—even if for more money or more recognition. I found this the strongest retention strategy to deploy. And hey, if they do move on to another role, isn't that (at least partially) to your credit? If you effectively create a space for them to grow, they will one day move on to greater things!

INTRODUCTION TO GENERATION Y (MILLENNIALS) AND GENERATION Z (ZOOMERS)

A seismic shift in the workforce has occurred over the past decade. In many ways, we now see this shift's implications play out in efforts to attract, develop, and retain the best of the available talent pool. Baby Boomers, who held key leadership roles, continue to phase out of the workforce in large numbers. Generation X can fill the potential leadership void; however, this group has a significantly smaller share of the current workforce. This puts a younger generation of workers in the driver's seat moving forward. Understanding the intricacies, dynamics, and impacts of Gen Y and Gen Z can help us strategically think about retaining high-potential workers and leaders while preserving our business legacy into the future.

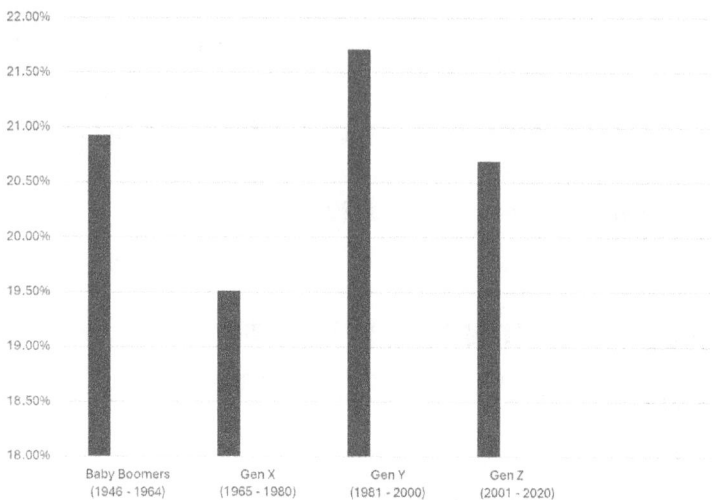

Figure 1. Workforce Generational Demographics

https://www.statista.com/statistics/296974/us-population
-share-by-generation/

https://www.bls.gov/opub/mlr/2015/article/labor-force
-projections-to-2024.htm

The two distinct cohorts of Generation Y, commonly known as Millennials, and Generation Z, often called Zoomers, have left an indelible mark on society, culture, and the workplace. As we delve into their characteristics, preferences, beliefs, and demographics, it becomes evident that while they share some similarities, each generation possesses its own unique traits and values.

Demographics (Figure 1): Generation Y, born between the early 1980s and mid-1990s, represents a sizable generation with a diverse demographic profile. They grew up in a world transitioning from analog to digital, and became first to witness the advent of the internet and mobile technology on a large scale. In contrast, Generation Z, born from the mid-1990s to the early

2010s, can be characterized as even more diverse and globally connected—true digital natives, born into a world where smartphones and social media had achieved a pervasive presence.

Technology and Connectivity: Millennials witnessed the rapid evolution of technology, adapting to the shift from dial-up internet to smartphones and social media, known for their tech-savviness, embracing digital tools and platforms. Zoomers, on the other hand, have mastered an innate digital fluency. They grew up in a hyperconnected world, navigating multiple screens effortlessly and consuming information in bite-sized, visual formats. Both generations strongly prefer online communication, making social media an integral part of their lives.

Work and Career Aspirations: Millennials entered the workforce during a period of economic turbulence, which influenced their career choices and values. They prioritize work-life balance, personal fulfillment, and purpose-driven careers. They seek employers who align with their values and provide opportunities for growth and development. Zoomers have just begun to enter the workforce but share similar values. They seek meaningful work, remain highly entrepreneurial, and value career flexibility. They likely prioritize job security and financial stability in response to the uncertainties they witnessed during their formative years.

Beliefs and Values: Both generations have a strong sense of social responsibility and a desire to positively impact the world. They feel passionately about social, economic, political, and environmental issues, often advocating and supporting brands that align with their values.

Education and Learning: Millennials pursued traditional education paths, valuing college degrees and structured learning.

Zoomers, however, continue to reshape education by embracing online learning platforms, self-directed learning, and alternative pathways to knowledge. They more likely prioritize practical skills and hands-on experience over formal education.

Global Perspective: Both generations have a global outlook, thanks to their internet and social media exposure. They hold awareness of global issues and more likely embrace multiculturalism. Growing up in an even more interconnected world, Zoomers remain particularly attuned to global events and issues.

Understanding Gen Y and Z is essential for individuals, businesses, and society at large. While each generation has unique characteristics and preferences, they share a common awareness of social dynamics and a tech-savvy nature. As they continue to shape the world, organizations and institutions must adapt to their evolving needs and values to effectively engage and empower these generations.

THE IMPACT OF SOCIETAL CHANGES ON THEIR WORLDVIEW

In today's dynamic and ever-evolving workplace, effective management, collaboration, and fostering a positive work environment depends on understanding the worldviews of different generations. Gen Y and Z have been at the forefront of recent societal changes, shaped by technological advancements, economic shifts, and cultural upheavals, all of which have significantly influenced their attitudes, values, and expectations in the workplace.

GENERATION Y: THE MILLENNIALS

DEFINING CHARACTERISTICS

Generation Y, commonly known as Millennials, refers to individuals born between approximately 1981 and 2000. This generation experienced a unique blend of analog and digital worlds during their formative years. They grew up witnessing the transition from dial-up internet to broadband, landline phones to smartphones, and traditional media to digital platforms.

1. **Technology Pioneers:** Millennials, often described as digital natives, became the first generation to fully embrace technology and the internet, shaping how we communicate, work, and live. This exposure to technology from a young age has influenced their worldview, making them tech-savvy and adaptable to rapid changes in the digital landscape.

2. **Optimistic and Ambitious:** Millennials grew up in a time of relative economic prosperity before experiencing the challenges of the 2008 financial crisis and its aftermath. As a result, they tend to be optimistic and ambitious, valuing personal and professional development.

3. **Value Work-Life Balance:** Unlike previous generations, Millennials prioritize work-life balance and value experiences over material possessions. They are more likely to seek flexible work arrangements, such as remote work or freelance opportunities, to align their careers with their personal lives.

4. **Embrace Innovation:** Millennials stay conscious of multiple perspectives and their contributions to new,

innovative ideas. They usually leverage this range of perspectives for a more well-rounded viewpoint. They expect their workplaces to be valued the same.

IMPACT OF SOCIETAL CHANGES ON MILLENNIAL WORLDVIEW

Several key societal changes have profoundly influenced the worldview of Millennial workers:

1. **Technology:** The rapid advancement of technology has shaped every aspect of Millennials' lives, including how they work and communicate. Accustomed to instant access to information, they hold a preference for quick decision-making and efficiency in the workplace.

2. **Economic Challenges:** Many Millennials entered the workforce during or after the 2008 financial crisis, making them cautious about financial stability. They tend to seek job security and financial well-being.

3. **Social Media:** The rise of social media has given Millennials a platform for self-expression and social activism. They more likely use social media to connect with peers, seek job opportunities, and express their opinions on workplace issues.

4. **Education:** Millennials tend to have higher education levels than previous generations, shaping their career expectations and making them more selective when choosing employers.

5. **Globalization:** Thanks to increased globalization, Millennials hold international perspectives and remain comfortable working in multicultural environments.

GENERATION Z: THE DIGITAL NATIVES

DEFINING CHARACTERISTICS

Gen Z represents individuals born roughly between 2001 and 2020, the first generation to grow up entirely in the digital age, with access to smartphones, social media, and instant connectivity from an early age.

1. **Tech-Integrated:** The most tech-integrated generation yet, Gen Z grew up with smartphones, tablets, and social media as integral parts of their lives, making them true digital natives, comfortable with various digital tools and platforms.

2. **Pragmatic and Entrepreneurial:** Marked by pragmatism and a strong entrepreneurial spirit, Gen Z seeks practical, career-oriented education, open to unconventional career paths, such as freelancing and gig work.

3. **Value Authenticity:** Authenticity is crucial to Gen Z. They value genuine interactions, honest communication, and brand authenticity, while quick to detect insincerity and value transparency in organizations.

4. **Global Citizens:** Gen Z has a global outlook, thanks to the internet and social media, making them more likely to identify as global citizens interested in global issues.

IMPACT OF SOCIETAL CHANGES ON GEN Z WORLDVIEW

Recent societal changes have significantly influenced Gen Z's worldview:

1. **Digital Dependency:** Growing up in a digital world has made Gen Z highly dependent on technology for communication, entertainment, and learning. They expect seamless technology integration in the workplace and may struggle in tech-averse environments.

2. **Economic Uncertainty:** Gen Z has witnessed economic volatility, including the 2008 financial crisis and the economic impact of the COVID-19 pandemic. As a result, they express caution about job security and financial stability.

3. **Information Overload:** The abundance of information and the constant stream of content on the internet have made Gen Z highly discerning information consumers. They value concise, relevant, and accurate communication in the workplace.

4. **Remote Work:** The COVID-19 pandemic accelerated the adoption of remote work, with Gen Z workers likely to continue seeking flexible work arrangements, valuing the freedom to work from anywhere.

BRIDGING THE GENERATIONAL DIVIDE IN THE WORKPLACE

To harness the strengths and perspectives of both Millennials and Gen Z in the workplace, organizations must navigate the generational divide effectively:

1. **Flexible Work Policies:** Offering flexible work arrangements, including remote work options, can accommodate the preferences of both generations and promote work-life balance.

2. **Mentorship Programs:** Establishing mentorship programs allow Gen Z employees to learn from experienced Millennial, Gen X, or even Baby Boomer colleagues, further facilitating knowledge transfer and skill development.

3. **Developmental Opportunities:** Providing consistent opportunities for professional growth and development to meet the Gen Y and Z deep desire to be constantly growing and improving. Being intentional with developmental opportunities and sharing how these contribute to their future in the organization, can have meaningful impact.

4. **Embrace Technology:** Embracing technology and providing continuous training to bridge the digital divide between generations can serve to encourage cross-generational collaboration in tech-related projects.

5. **Effective Communication:** Tailoring communication strategies to the preferences of each generation means

respecting the Gen Z preference for concise and visual communication, and Millennials appreciation of in-depth discussions.

Understanding the worldview of Gen Y and Z employees marks an essential tactic for organizations to thrive in the modern world. These generations have been shaped by unique societal changes, including technological advancements, economic challenges, and cultural shifts. By recognizing their distinct characteristics and values, organizations can create adaptable and forward-thinking workplaces that benefit from the strengths of both generations and ensure long-term success in an ever-evolving business landscape.

KEY GENERATIONAL DIFFERENCES AND SIMILARITIES

In retaining Gen Y and Z employees, employers must recognize the commonalities and differences defining these generations. While they share a strong affinity for technology, a desire for meaningful work, and a commitment to innovation, they also have unique characteristics and priorities. By tailoring retention strategies to accommodate these similarities and differences, organizations can create environments that engage, empower, and retain Gen Y and Z talent, ensuring a dynamic and successful future workforce.

1. **Technology Natives:** One striking similarity between Gen Y and Z remains their status as technology natives. Both generations have grown up in a digital world, with access to the internet and smartphones from a young age. This shared digital fluency manifests in their comfort with technology, preference for digital communication, and adaptability to rapidly

changing tech landscapes. Employers must recognize this commonality and leverage technology to engage and connect with these generations through remote work options, digital training platforms, or virtual collaboration tools.

2. **Desire for Meaningful Work:** Gen Y and Z share a common desire for meaningful work. They seek roles that align with their values and allow them to positively impact the world. Both generations value purpose-driven careers and are likelier to stay with organizations prioritizing new ideas and perspectives. Employers can retain these employees by fostering a sense of purpose and emphasizing how their roles contribute to broader organizational strategy.

3. **Desire for Growth:** Both generations will not tolerate stagnation. They want genuinely willing leaders to invest in their personal and professional development. They want to share aspirations and goals with their leaders and feel known and recognized for their efforts and ambitions. Employers must think strategically about developmental opportunities, including seminars, leader development programs, lateral promotions, special projects, or temporary leadership opportunities.

4. **Flexible Work Arrangements:** Gen Y and Z share a preference for flexible work arrangements. They value work-life balance and seek jobs that offer remote or flexible work options. The events of the COVID-19 pandemic further underscored the importance of such arrangements. Employers can retain these employees by offering flexibility in work hours and locations, allowing for better work and personal life integration.

5. **Unique Characteristics:** While Gen Y and Z share these commonalities, they also have unique characteristics that distinguish them from each other:

   › **Gen Y:** Often called digital pioneers, these people came of age during the transition from analog to digital technology. They tend to value experiences, such as travel and adventure, and prioritize work-life balance. They are more likely to appreciate traditional career paths and stability.

   › **Gen Z:** As true digital natives, this group has been immersed in technology from birth, characterized by their entrepreneurial spirit, adaptability, and comfort with change. They value financial stability and security, having grown up during economic uncertainties, and more likely embrace non-linear career paths while prioritizing financial well-being.

SUMMARY OF CHAPTER 2: UNDERSTANDING THE GENERATIONS

Chapter 2 examines the unique characteristics, preferences, and values of Generation Y (Millennials) and Generation Z (Zoomers), two generational cohorts shaping the modern workforce. Millennials, born between the early 1980s and mid-1990s, and Gen Z, born from the mid-1990s to early 2010s, both hold a deep affinity for technology, a strong desire for meaningful work, and a shared commitment to innovation and social responsibility. However, their formative experiences and priorities also reveal distinct differences.

- **Millennials** grew up witnessing the digital revolution, bridging the gap between analog and digital technologies. This makes them adaptable, optimistic, and focused on work-life balance. They value traditional career paths, structured learning, and alignment with organizational values.

- **Gen Z**, having grown up in a fully digital world, displays an innate digital fluency, entrepreneurial spirit, and adaptability to change. They prioritize authenticity, financial security, and practical skills over formal education.

- **Both generations** emphasize purpose-driven careers, global awareness, and flexibility in work arrangements. Millennials entered the workforce during economic turbulence, making them cautious about financial stability, while Gen Z experienced global crises like COVID-19 during their formative years, further reinforcing their pragmatic approach to careers and finances.

Organizations must understand these dynamics to effectively engage and retain these generations. Strategies such as fostering purpose, leveraging technology, offering growth opportunities, and ensuring flexible work arrangements are critical to meeting their expectations.

While their shared characteristics create common ground, their differences demand tailored approaches. By addressing the unique needs of Millennials and Gen Z, employers can create inclusive, innovative, and future-ready workplaces that attract and retain top talent.

KEY BULLET POINTS

- **Generational Demographics:** Millennials represent 21.71% of the U.S. population, while Gen Z accounts for 20.69%.
- **Technology Affinity:** Both generations are technology natives; Millennials adapted to digital, while Gen Z grew up immersed in it.
- **Workplace Priorities:** Both value meaningful work, flexibility, and alignment with organizational values.
- **Millennial Characteristics:** Optimistic, work-life balance-focused, and driven by structured career paths.
- **Gen Z Characteristics:** Entrepreneurial, authenticity-seeking, and pragmatic about financial security.

- **Education and Skills:** Millennials prioritize formal education, while Gen Z embraces practical, hands-on learning.
- **Global Awareness:** Both generations are socially and globally conscious, advocating for inclusivity and sustainability.
- **Retention Strategies:** Flexible work policies, mentorship programs, and growth opportunities are vital to engaging both generations.

KEY SKILLS AND APPROACHES

- **Adaptability:** Recognize and respond to the dynamic needs of a tech-savvy, socially conscious workforce.
- **Mentorship:** Create programs that bridge the generational divide, encouraging knowledge transfer and collaboration.
- **Technology Integration:** Provide tools and training that enhance digital fluency and support innovation.
- **Flexibility:** Offer remote work and flexible schedules to align with work-life balance priorities.
- **Purpose-Driven Leadership:** Emphasize the organization's mission and its alignment with employees' values.
- **Growth Opportunities:** Invest in professional development programs tailored to personal and career aspirations.

QUESTIONS TO DEEPEN UNDERSTANDING

1. How can organizations balance the shared values of Millennials and Gen Z with their unique characteristics?
2. What role does technology play in fostering engagement and productivity for these generations?
3. How can mentorship programs help bridge generational divides and encourage collaboration?

4. What specific steps can organizations take to provide meaningful career growth for Millennials and Gen Z?

5. How do the economic experiences of these generations influence their career priorities and decision-making?

6. What strategies can organizations adopt to foster authenticity and trust with Gen Z employees?

7. How can global awareness and social responsibility be incorporated into organizational culture to attract these generations?

8. What lessons can older generations of leaders learn from the perspectives and priorities of Millennials and Gen Z?

CHAPTER 3

THE CHANGING LANDSCAPE OF WORK

THE EXECUTIVE VIEWPOINT

Nate Smith
Alliant Insurance Services, First Vice President, Data
Security
TOPIC: How Remote Work Improves Gen Y and Gen Z
Employees

As a member of Generation Y who has spent several years working remotely, I have seen firsthand how this mode of work can significantly improve employee retention, particularly among Gen Y and Z. Remote work has evolved from being a mere recruiting tool to a crucial strategy for retaining and engaging employees. However, the recent push by some companies to bring remote workers back into the office might backfire, causing many employees to seek out organizations that offer the flexibility they have come to value. While hybrid work environments are emerging as a potential solution, their effectiveness in maintaining employee satisfaction and retention remains uncertain.

One of the primary reasons behind the effectiveness of remote work in retaining Gen Y and Z employees comes via the flexibility it offers. These generations place a high value on work-life balance and the ability to manage their own schedules. According to a 2021 FlexJobs survey, 58% of respondents said they would "absolutely" look for a new job if they couldn't continue remote work. This statistic underscores how crucial remote work has become in the job market. From my own experience, the ability to work remotely has allowed me to better balance my professional and personal responsibilities, leading to increased job satisfaction and loyalty to my employer.

Remote work also eliminates the daily commute, which can be a significant source of stress and time consumption. According to the U.S. Census Bureau, the average one-way commute time in the U.S. is 27.6 minutes. By working remotely, employees can save nearly an hour each day, which can be redirected towards more productive or personally fulfilling activities. This time savings can contribute to higher productivity and better mental health, both of which are crucial for long-term employee retention.

Moreover, remote work can reduce overhead costs for employers, which can be reinvested in employee benefits and development opportunities. Companies that have embraced remote work often report lower expenses related to office space, utilities, and supplies. This financial flexibility allows them to offer competitive salaries, comprehensive benefits packages, and opportunities for professional growth—factors that are highly valued by Gen Y and Z employees. In my own career, I have seen how companies that prioritize employee development and well-being can foster a more loyal and engaged workforce.

However, the current trend of companies attempting to bring remote workers back to the office remains concerning. This move can be perceived as a step backward, particularly for those who have thrived in a remote work environment. The risk is that employees, particularly those from Gen Y and Z who have experienced the benefits of remote work, will seek employment elsewhere. According to a 2022 Gallup survey, 54% of employees who prefer remote work would likely look for another job if required to return to the office full-time. This statistic highlights the potential consequences of enforcing a return to the office without considering employee preferences.

Hybrid work environments, which combine remote and in-office work, are being explored as a middle ground. While this approach offers some flexibility, its long-term effectiveness in retaining employees is still unknown. There are concerns about how hybrid work might impact team cohesion, communication, and overall productivity. However, if implemented thoughtfully, hybrid models could offer a balance that satisfies both employer and employee needs.

In conclusion, remote work has proven to be a powerful tool for improving employee retention, particularly among Gen Y and Z. These generations highly value the flexibility, time savings, and enhanced work-life balance it offers. Companies should carefully consider the potential negative impact of mandating a return to the office and explore hybrid work models as a possible compromise. As someone who has benefited greatly from remote work, I firmly believe that embracing this trend can lead to a more satisfied and loyal workforce.

> **Interesting fact:** *Two-thirds of Gen Zs (64 percent) and Millennials (66 percent) say they work for organizations that have recently implemented a return-to-office policy, calling people back to the office full-time or part-time. Overall, a narrow majority of respondents now work fully on-site (51 percent of Gen Zs and 57 percent of Millennials). Only 15 percent of Gen Zs and 11 percent of Millennials work fully remote, with another third of Gen Zs (35 percent) and Millennials (33 percent) working hybrid. While return-to-office mandates have yielded mixed results, it's clear that Gen Zs and Millennials continue to value flexible work in terms of when and where they work. This drive for greater flexibility seems to increase the popularity of less traditional employment models. For example, continuing a trend that emerged in last year's report, Gen Zs and Millennials would like employers to create more part-time jobs and job-sharing options and*

EVOLUTION OF WORK AND WORKPLACES IN THE 21ST CENTURY

The 21st century has witnessed a profound transformation in work and workplaces. Technological advancements, demographic shifts, globalization, and changing societal values have all contributed to the evolving work landscape. This chapter explores the key trends and developments that have shaped how we work and the environments in which we work.

THE DIGITAL REVOLUTION: TRANSFORMING THE NATURE OF WORK

At the heart of the 21st-century workplace evolution stands the digital revolution. The rapid advancement of technology has redefined how work is performed, accessed, and managed. Some key aspects of this transformation include:

1. **Remote Work and Telecommuting:** The rise of high-speed internet, cloud computing, and collaboration tools has made remote work a viable and attractive option for many employees. Telecommuting allows individuals to work from anywhere, blurring the boundaries between work and personal life. The COVID-19 pandemic accelerated this trend, with remote work becoming the norm for numerous industries.

2. **Automation and Artificial Intelligence (AI):**
   Automation and AI technologies have automated
   routine tasks across various industries. While they can
   potentially increase efficiency and productivity, they have
   also raised concerns about job displacement. The 21st
   century has seen a shift in the types of skills and roles in
   demand, with a growing emphasis on problem-solving,
   creativity, and digital literacy.

3. **Gig Economy and Freelancing:** The gig economy,
   characterized by short-term contracts and freelance
   work, has gained prominence. Platforms like Uber,
   Airbnb, and Upwork have provided opportunities
   for independent work, offering flexibility and raising
   questions about job security and worker rights.

CHANGING WORKFORCE DEMOGRAPHICS

Demographic shifts have had a significant impact on the workforce composition and workplace dynamics:

1. **Multigenerational Workforce:** The workplace now
   includes multiple generations, from Baby Boomers to
   Generation Z. Each generation brings its own set of
   values, expectations, and communication preferences,
   leading to a need for effective intergenerational
   collaboration.

2. **Aging Workforce:** As life expectancy increases,
   a larger proportion of the workforce approaches
   retirement age. This has led to discussions about
   talent retention, knowledge transfer, and strategies for
   accommodating older workers.

3. **Generation Z:** Digital Natives: Generation Z, born in the late 1990s and early 2000s, represents the first true generation of digital natives. Their technological proficiency and expectations for flexible, tech-integrated workplaces continue to reshape organizational cultures.

GLOBALIZATION AND REMOTE COLLABORATION

Globalization has expanded business horizons and increased the need for cross-border collaboration. International teams, diverse cultures, and the ability to connect and collaborate with colleagues and clients worldwide characterize the 21st-century workplace. Virtual communication tools and video conferencing have made it possible to work seamlessly across different time zones and geographies.

THE RISE OF WORK-LIFE INTEGRATION

Work-life balance has evolved into work-life integration as employees seek ways to harmonize their personal and professional lives. They do not necessarily expect to separate work and personal time, but to find a balance allowing them to fulfill their responsibilities at work and home.

FLEXIBLE WORK ARRANGEMENTS

The 21st-century workplace recognizes that one size does not fit all. Employers increasingly offer flexible work arrangements, including part-time work, compressed workweeks, job sharing, and sabbaticals, to accommodate diverse employee needs and preferences.

WELLNESS AND MENTAL HEALTH INITIATIVES

Organizations have recognized the importance of employee well-being and have introduced wellness programs, mental health support, and stress management initiatives. The workplace has become a space not only for productivity but also for nurturing physical and mental health.

THE AGILE AND COLLABORATIVE WORKSPACE

Traditional cubicles and fixed office spaces give way to open-plan offices, co-working spaces, and flexible layouts that encourage collaboration and innovation. These designs prioritize adaptability and employee comfort.

THE ROLE OF LEADERSHIP IN WORKPLACE EVOLUTION

Leaders in the 21st-century workplace must adapt to these changes by fostering a culture of adaptability, continuous learning, and resilience. Effective leadership involves understanding a multigenerational workforce's diverse needs and expectations, while providing clear communication and support.

THE FUTURE OF WORK AND WORKPLACE EVOLUTION

The 21st century has laid the groundwork for continued evolution in the world of work. Emerging technologies like augmented reality (AR), virtual reality (VR), and blockchain stand ready to further reshape industries and job roles. As the global economy becomes increasingly interconnected, organizations will need to navigate challenges related to data security, privacy, and the ethical use of technology.

The 21st century has ushered in a new era of work and workplaces. The digital revolution, changing demographics, globalization, and shifting values have transformed how, where, and why we work. Organizations and individuals must remain adaptable, embrace technological advancements, prioritize employee well-being, and champion the inclusion of all perspectives and backgrounds to thrive in this evolving landscape. The future of work promises exciting opportunities and challenges, making it essential to stay agile and prepared for what lies ahead.

THE RISE OF REMOTE AND FLEXIBLE WORK ARRANGEMENTS

The workplace landscape has undergone a seismic shift in recent years, with the rise of remote work and flexible work arrangements. This transformation, accelerated by technological advancements and changing societal norms, has brought numerous benefits for employers and employees. In this review, we will explore how adopting remote and flexible work arrangements not only reshapes how we work but also plays a pivotal role in retaining Generation Y (Millennials) and Generation Z (Zoomers) employees. We will explore the advantages of remote work and flexibility for these younger generations, shedding light on why these arrangements are becoming indispensable in the modern workplace.

32% of workers report wanting to continue working remotely. (*Forbes Advisor, 2024*)

UNDERSTANDING REMOTE WORK AND FLEXIBLE WORK ARRANGEMENTS

Remote work occurs outside the traditional office, often from home or other remote locations. Flexible work arrangements encompass various strategies, such as flextime, compressed workweeks, and job sharing, allowing employees greater control over when and where they work. Both remote work and flexible arrangements continue to rise, with an increasingly evident impact on workforce retention.

ENHANCED WORK-LIFE BALANCE

A primary reason remote and flexible work arrangements resonate with Gen Y and Z can be found in the promise of enhanced work-life balance. These generations value experiences and personal fulfillment as much as their careers. Remote work allows them to better integrate their professional and personal lives, reducing commute times and providing the flexibility to attend to personal responsibilities without sacrificing job performance. The ability to work when and where it's most convenient empowers them to prioritize self-care, family, and personal pursuits, ultimately fostering a happier and more engaged workforce.

IMPROVED JOB SATISFACTION AND ENGAGEMENT

Job satisfaction and engagement represent critical factors in employee retention. Millennials and Gen Z thrive in work environments that offer autonomy and trust. Remote work allows them to manage their tasks and schedules, contributing to a sense of ownership over their work. With the right technology and communication tools, they can collaborate effectively with colleagues and supervisors, mitigating concerns about isolation. Additionally, eliminating the daily commute can significantly reduce stress and burnout, increasing job satisfaction and retention rates.

ACCESS TO A GLOBAL TALENT POOL

Remote work breaks down geographic barriers, allowing organizations to tap into a global talent pool. For Gen Y and Z employees, this means access to a broader range of job opportunities. They can seek positions that align with their skills and interests rather than being constrained by geographical location. The ability to work remotely also opens doors to diverse and inclusive workforces, highly valued by younger generations. Companies that embrace remote work can attract and retain top talent worldwide, contributing to their competitive advantage.

FLEXIBILITY FOR LIFELONG LEARNING

The desire for continuous learning and skill development offers a defining characteristic of Gen Y and Z. Remote work and flexible arrangements enable these employees to pursue education, training, and personal development opportunities more easily. Whether taking online courses, attending workshops, or acquiring new certifications, remote work offers the time and flexibility necessary to invest in their professional growth. Employers that support these pursuits empower their employees and benefit from a more skilled and adaptable workforce.

REDUCED COMMUTE STRESS

Commuting can be a significant source of stress and unproductive time for younger employees. Eliminating or reducing the need for daily commutes, remote work, and flexible arrangements contributes to lower stress levels and better mental health.

The rise of remote work and flexible work arrangements represents a transformative shift in the workplace, with profound implications for retaining Generation Y and Generation Z employees. These arrangements offer enhanced work-life balance, improved job satisfaction and engagement, access to a global talent pool, flexibility for lifelong learning, and reduced commute-related stress and environmental impact. By recognizing and embracing the preferences and values of these younger generations, organizations can position themselves as employers of choice and gain a competitive edge in the modern workforce. As remote work evolves, its impact on workforce retention will remain a critical topic for HR professionals and executive leaders.

TECHNOLOGICAL ADVANCEMENTS AND THEIR INFLUENCE ON WORK

Recent technological advancements have ushered in a profound transformation across all business sectors and have fundamentally reshaped the workplace for employees and organizations. Here's how these advancements have changed the workplace for everyone:

1. **Digital Transformation:** Technology has enabled the digitalization of processes, data, and communication in virtually every industry. This digital transformation has streamlined operations, reduced paper-based workflows, and increased the speed and efficiency of tasks.

2. **Remote Work and Telecommuting:** The advent of high-speed internet, cloud computing, and collaboration tools has made remote work a reality for many employees. This flexibility has allowed individuals to work from anywhere, leading to more geographically dispersed workforces.

3. **Automation and AI:** Artificial intelligence (AI) and automation technologies have revolutionized industries by automating routine tasks and enhancing decision-making processes. This has led to increased productivity and efficiency but has also raised questions about job displacement.

4. **Virtual Reality (VR) and Augmented Reality (AR):** VR and AR technologies create training, design, and immersive experiences. In manufacturing, healthcare, and education sectors, these technologies transform how employees learn and interact with their environments.

5. **Data Analytics:** Big data and advanced analytics help businesses make data-driven decisions, with implications for marketing, customer service, supply chain management, and financial analysis.

6. **Cybersecurity:** The increased reliance on digital systems has necessitated a focus on cybersecurity. Companies continue investing in cybersecurity measures to protect sensitive data and maintain trust with customers and clients.

7. **Communication Tools:** Communication tools like video conferencing, messaging apps, and collaboration platforms have facilitated real-time communication and remote collaboration. They have become essential for distributed teams and global organizations.

8. **E-commerce and Online Shopping:** The rise of e-commerce platforms has disrupted traditional

retail, changed consumer behavior, and created new opportunities for businesses to reach customers online.

9. **Healthcare Telemedicine:** Telemedicine has become more prevalent, allowing patients to consult with healthcare providers remotely. This has proven especially important during public health crises.

10. **Education Technology (EdTech):** Technology has revolutionized education, enabling online learning, personalized instruction, and the use of interactive tools for both students and educators.

11. **Sustainability and Energy Efficiency:** Advancements in technology have facilitated the adoption of sustainable practices, from energy-efficient buildings to renewable energy sources and eco-friendly manufacturing processes.

12. **Supply Chain Optimization:** Technology integration has improved supply chain management, allowing for better inventory control, demand forecasting, and logistics optimization.

13. **Customer Experience:** Technology has enabled businesses to provide personalized and seamless customer experiences through data analytics, AI-driven recommendations, and chatbots.

14. **Financial Technology (FinTech):** The financial sector has seen the rise of FinTech, transforming banking, payments, and investment services with online platforms and digital currencies.

15. **Entertainment and Streaming:** The entertainment industry has shifted toward digital streaming platforms, changing how people access and consume content, from music to movies and television.

16. **Social Media and Marketing:** Social media platforms have become vital for marketing and customer engagement. They offer businesses new ways to connect with audiences and gather data on consumer preferences.

17. **Sustainability Reporting:** Technology has made it easier for companies to track and report their environmental, social, and governance (ESG) efforts, reflecting the growing importance of sustainability in business.

These technological advancements have touched virtually every aspect of the workplace, from how tasks are performed to how teams collaborate and how businesses interact with customers. They have created new opportunities and challenges, requiring organizations and employees to continually adapt and evolve to remain competitive in an increasingly digital world.

ARTIFICIAL INTELLIGENCE—THE IMPACT ON RETAINING EMPLOYEES

Artificial Intelligence (AI) has brought about significant changes in the workplace across various industries and functions. Its impact is transformative, touching on everything from productivity and decision-making to automation and job roles. AI has changed the workplace in these key areas:

1. **Automation of Routine Tasks:** AI-powered automation tools can perform repetitive, rule-based

tasks more efficiently than humans. This has led to automating tasks such as data entry, document processing, and routine customer service inquiries, freeing up employees to focus on higher-value work.

2. **Enhanced Decision-Making:** AI systems can analyze vast amounts of data quickly and accurately. This capability aids decision-making by providing valuable insights and predictions. In finance, healthcare, and marketing sectors, AI-powered analytic tools assist professionals in making data-driven decisions.

3. **Personalization:** AI enables personalization at scale. For example, AI algorithms analyze customer data to tailor product recommendations and marketing messages to individual preferences. This personalization enhances customer experiences.

4. **Customer Service and Chatbots:** AI-powered chatbots and virtual assistants increasingly address customer service and support, handling routine customer queries, providing product information, troubleshooting, improving response times, and reducing customer service workloads.

5. **Predictive Maintenance:** In industries like manufacturing and transportation, AI-driven predictive maintenance analyzes equipment sensor data to forecast when machinery needs maintenance or repairs. This minimizes downtime and reduces maintenance costs.

6. **Natural Language Processing (NLP):** NLP technology enables machines to understand and respond to human

language. This has applications in customer service chatbots, virtual assistants, language translation, and sentiment analysis of customer feedback.

7. **Human Resources:** HR uses AI for resume screening, candidate sourcing, and employee onboarding. It also can predict employee attrition and help identify areas for employee development.

8. **Healthcare Diagnostics:** In healthcare, AI performs medical imaging analysis, disease diagnosis, drug discovery, and patient data management. AI algorithms can assist healthcare professionals in diagnosing conditions more accurately and quickly.

9. **Supply Chain Optimization:** AI helps supply chain management by forecasting demand, improving inventory management, and optimizing logistics routes. This leads to cost savings and increased efficiency.

10. **Cybersecurity:** AI detects and responds to cybersecurity threats in real-time. It can identify abnormal network activity, detect malware, and enhance security.

11. **Education and eLearning:** AI used in personalized learning platforms adapts content and assessments to individual student needs. This improves educational outcomes by catering to each student's pace and learning style.

12. **Content Creation and Curation:** AI can generate content, such as news articles or reports, based on

data and templates. It is also used to curate content for websites and social media platforms.

13. **Financial Services:** AI-driven robo-advisors provide automated investment advice and portfolio management. AI algorithms analyze market trends and financial data to make investment recommendations.

14. **Virtual Reality (VR) and Augmented Reality (AR):** AI enhances both the VR and AR experiences by enabling more realistic simulations and interactions used in training, education, and entertainment.

15. **Ethical Considerations:** AI has introduced ethical considerations in the workplace, including issues related to bias in AI algorithms, privacy concerns, and the impact of automation on job displacement.

While AI has brought numerous benefits to the workplace, it has also raised questions about job roles, employee training, ethical use, and the need for regulations to ensure responsible AI deployment. Organizations must carefully navigate these changes to harness the full potential of AI while addressing associated challenges.

Using AI to retain Gen Y and Z employees requires a strategic approach that leverages technology to address their unique preferences and needs. Here are several ways AI can be utilized for this purpose:

1. **Personalized Learning and Development:** AI-driven learning platforms can create personalized training and development plans for each employee based on their skills, goals, and learning style. This helps Gen

Y and Z employees feel that their professional growth has been supported and tailored to their needs.

2. **Skill Assessment and Career Pathing:** AI can assess employees' skills and competencies and recommend suitable career paths within the organization. This proactive approach demonstrates the company's commitment to career progression and development.

3. **Mentorship Matching:** AI algorithms can match employees with suitable mentors or peer mentors within the organization. Providing mentorship opportunities aligns with the desire for professional growth and learning among younger generations.

4. **Feedback and Performance Management:** AI-powered performance management tools can provide continuous feedback and insights to employees and managers. Real-time feedback aligns with Gen Y and Z's desire for regular communication and growth-oriented feedback.

5. **Predictive Analytics for Attrition Risk:** AI can analyze data to identify employees at risk of leaving the organization. By proactively addressing concerns or providing retention incentives, employers can reduce turnover among these generations.

6. **Employee Well-being Support:** AI chatbots or virtual assistants can provide mental health and well-being resources and support, to include stress management tips, mindfulness exercises, or access to employee assistance programs.

7. **Flexible Work Arrangements:** AI can help manage and optimize flexible work arrangements, ensuring that remote work schedules remain fair, and employees have the tools to work effectively from anywhere.

8. **Predictive Hiring:** AI can assist in identifying those candidates during the hiring process likely to thrive in the organization's culture, reducing the likelihood of poor cultural fits and subsequent turnover.

9. **Employee Engagement Surveys:** AI can analyze employee engagement survey responses to identify trends and areas that need attention. This enables organizations to take targeted actions to improve workplace satisfaction.

10. **Automated Onboarding:** AI can streamline onboarding by automating administrative tasks, providing new employees with resources and information, and ensuring a smoother transition into the organization.

11. **Work-Life Balance:** AI can help employees manage their work-life balance by providing tools to schedule and prioritize tasks effectively, reducing stress related to workload management.

12. **Internal Communication:** AI-powered chatbots and virtual assistants can answer common employee questions, making it easier for employees to find information and stay updated about company policies and updates.

13. **Recognition and Rewards:** AI can track employee achievements and recommend appropriate recognition and rewards. This ensures that accomplishments receive the proper acknowledgement.

Using AI to complement human interactions rather than replace them is essential. AI should support HR and leadership efforts in creating a workplace culture that aligns with the preferences and needs of Gen Y and Z employees, fostering a sense of belonging, growth, and purpose within the organization. Additionally, organizations should be transparent about the use of AI and ensure that data privacy and ethical considerations receive the proper level of attention.

THE GIG ECONOMY AND ITS APPEAL TO YOUNGER GENERATIONS

The gig economy describes a labor market characterized by short-term contracts, freelance work, temporary positions, and independent contractor arrangements rather than traditional, long-term employment. It allows individuals to work on a project-by-project basis, often with multiple clients or employers, giving them more flexibility and autonomy.

The gig economy has gained significant appeal among younger generations, including Gen Y and Z, for several reasons:

1. **Flexibility:** The gig economy provides a high degree of flexibility regarding work hours and location. Millennials and Gen Z highly value work-life balance and the ability to control their schedules. Gig work allows them to adapt their work to their personal lives, making it an attractive option.

2. **Autonomy:** Independent gig workers have more control over the type of work they take on and how they perform it. This autonomy aligns with the desire for self-determination many younger generations seek in their careers.

3. **Diverse Opportunities:** Gig work spans various industries and job types, from freelance writing and graphic design to ride-sharing and food delivery. This diversity of opportunities appeals to individuals with various skill sets and interests.

4. **Entrepreneurial Spirit:** Many younger workers possess an entrepreneurial spirit and a desire to be their own bosses. The gig economy allows them to test and develop their entrepreneurial ideas while earning income.

5. **Skills Development:** Gig work often requires individuals to wear multiple hats, manage their finances, market themselves, and handle client interactions. This can lead to skill development and a broader skill set, which can be valuable for future career opportunities.

6. **Side Hustles:** For some, gig work is a side hustle in addition to traditional employment. This supplementary income can help individuals pay off debt, save for goals, or pursue personal interests.

7. **Portfolio Careers:** Younger generations remain increasingly open to portfolio careers, where they combine multiple gig roles or freelance projects to

create a diverse income stream. This approach allows them to explore different interests and passions.

8. **Technology Integration:** The gig economy relies heavily on platforms and apps connecting freelancers with clients or customers. The younger generations, as digital natives, take great comfort in technology for communication and work management.

9. **Access to a Global Marketplace:** The internet and digital platforms have enabled gig workers to access a global marketplace. They can collaborate with clients or customers worldwide, broadening their professional network.

10. **Social Responsibility:** Some gig workers appreciate the opportunity to work for companies or platforms that align with their values and beliefs, particularly regarding environmental sustainability or social impact.

While the gig economy offers numerous benefits, it also comes with challenges, such as income volatility, lack of job security, and limited access to traditional employment benefits like health insurance and retirement plans. As a result, many younger workers engage in gig work as part of a diverse career strategy, combining gig opportunities with traditional employment to balance income stability and flexibility.

HOW WORK-LIFE INTEGRATION RESHAPES CAREER EXPECTATIONS

Work-life integration profoundly reshapes career expectations for Gen Y and Z, fundamentally altering how they approach their professional lives. Examples of how work-life integration impacts the career expectations of these younger generations follows:

1. **Flexible Work Arrangements:** Gen Y and Z prioritize flexibility in their work arrangements. They seek employers who offer options for remote work, flexible hours, and the ability to tailor their work schedules to accommodate personal commitments. They expect work to fit around their lives rather than the other way around.

2. **Balancing Personal and Professional Goals:** Both generations focus more on balancing personal and professional goals. They are less willing to sacrifice personal time, family, and leisure for their careers. As a result, they expect employers to respect and support this balance.

3. **Rejection of the "Always On" Culture:** Gen Y and Z challenge the traditional notion of being constantly "on the clock," clearly less likely to accept a culture of working late into the evening or over weekends as a badge of honor. Instead, they value clear boundaries between work and personal time, aiming for productivity during work hours and restorative time afterward.

4. **Focus on Meaningful Work:** Younger generations highly value meaningful work that aligns with their values. They expect their careers to have a purpose beyond just financial gain. They more likely seek employers prioritizing social responsibility and sustainability.

5. **Job Mobility:** Gen Y and Z demonstrate more openness to changing jobs and employers if their current workplace does not meet their expectations for work-life integration. They value job mobility to finding a better fit, and may not stay in roles that compromise their quality of life.

6. **Entrepreneurial Pursuits:** Many individuals from these generations find themselves drawn to entrepreneurship and self-employment because it allows them to have greater control over their work schedules and work-life balance. The gig economy and freelancing also align with their desire for autonomy.

7. **Technology as an Enabler:** Technology integration plays a pivotal role in work-life integration. This generation is comfortable using digital tools to manage work tasks efficiently and stay connected to work outside the office. Technology enables remote work, virtual collaboration, and greater work-life harmony.

8. **Mental Health and Well-being:** Mental health and well-being stand as paramount considerations for Gen Y and Z. They prioritize employers that support their mental and emotional health, offering resources and initiatives to manage stress and burnout and maintain a healthy work-life balance.

9. **Expectation of Remote Work:** The COVID-19 pandemic accelerated the acceptance of remote work as a viable option. Gen Y and Z now expect remote work to be offered, at least in part, by employers. They see it as gaining control over their work environment and daily routines.

Work-life integration redefines career expectations for Gen Y and Z by emphasizing flexibility, balance, meaningful work, and mental well-being. These generations continue to drive a shift toward more human-centered workplaces, and employers who adapt to these changing expectations stand a greater chance of attracting and retaining top talent from these cohorts.

SUMMARY OF CHAPTER 3: THE CHANGING LANDSCAPE OF WORK

Chapter 3 explores how work and workplaces have transformed in the 21st century, emphasizing the pivotal role of technology, shifting generational values, globalization, and societal changes. The chapter delves into how these forces shape workforce dynamics, employee expectations, and organizational practices.

- **Generational shifts** are transformative. Millennials (Gen Y) and Zoomers (Gen Z) comprise a significant portion of the workforce and prioritize work-life integration, meaningful work, and mental well-being. They reject rigid work structures, favoring remote or hybrid work and demanding purpose-driven careers. Remote work surged during the COVID-19 pandemic, fostering flexibility in balancing professional and personal lives.

- **Globalization and technology** have allowed businesses to harness talent worldwide, evolving the workplace from static cubicles to agile, collaborative spaces, fostering innovation and creativity. Organizations increasingly prioritize employee well-being, introducing wellness and mental health support programs. Employers that embrace these preferences and foster inclusive, adaptive cultures position themselves as leaders in attracting and retaining top talent.

- **AI and technology** enable flexible work management, personalized learning, and predictive analytics to prevent attrition, aligning organizational practices with employee expectations. Automation and AI have streamlined routine tasks but also raised concerns about job displacement, emphasizing the need for skills like problem-solving and creativity.

- **The gig economy** has great appeal to Gen Y and Z, highlighting its flexibility, autonomy, and entrepreneurial opportunities. Despite its challenges, such as income instability and lack of benefits, the gig economy reflects younger generations' desire for diverse, purpose-driven careers.

This evolving landscape presents opportunities and challenges, requiring organizations to remain agile and responsive. By understanding and addressing the unique needs of modern employees, businesses can thrive in this era of unprecedented change.

KEY BULLET POINTS

- **Digital Transformation:** Remote work, automation, and AI are reshaping workplace practices.
- **Generational Impact:** Gen Y and Z prioritize flexibility, purpose, and well-being in their careers.
- **Globalization:** Cross-border collaboration is enabled by technology and diverse workforces.
- **Work-life Integration:** Younger generations value careers that accommodate personal and professional goals.

- **AI in the Workplace:** AI facilitates personalized learning, employee engagement, and attrition prevention.
- **Gig Economy:** Offers autonomy and flexibility but presents challenges like income instability.
- **Wellness Focus:** Organizations prioritize mental health and employee well-being to enhance retention.
- **Future of Work:** Emerging technologies like AR, VR, and blockchain promise continued workplace evolution.

KEY SKILLS AND APPROACHES

- **Adaptability:** Embrace technological advancements and changing employee expectations.
- **Flexibility:** Offer remote, hybrid, and alternative work arrangements to align with workforce demands.
- **Purpose-Driven Leadership:** Cultivate a culture that values meaningful work and organizational alignment.
- **AI Integration:** Leverage AI for personalized development, predictive analytics, and flexible work management.
- **Wellness Initiatives:** Support mental health through programs, resources, and policies.
- **Global Collaboration:** Develop cross-cultural competencies to navigate international teamwork effectively.
- **Entrepreneurial Mindset:** Encourage innovation and autonomy to engage Gen Y and Z employees.

QUESTIONS FOR DEEPER UNDERSTANDING

1. How can organizations effectively balance flexibility and productivity in remote and hybrid work models?
2. What strategies can businesses use to address concerns about job displacement due to automation and AI?
3. How can organizations tailor their wellness initiatives to meet the needs of multigenerational workforces?

4. What role does work-life integration play in retaining top talent from Gen Y and Z?
5. How can leaders foster collaboration and cohesion in increasingly global and virtual teams?
6. What are the key benefits and risks of embracing the gig economy as part of a workforce strategy?
7. How can AI be utilized ethically to enhance employee engagement and career development?
8. What lessons from the gig economy can traditional organizations apply to improve flexibility and autonomy?
9. How can businesses ensure that their use of emerging technology aligns with their employees' evolving expectations?

CHAPTER 4

THE THREE FORCES OF EMPLOYEE RETENTION

Jason Morwick
MacRae Business Solutions, Inc.
CEO & President
TOPIC: Future Strategies to Improve Retention of Top Talent

In conversations with organizational leaders, most agree that their people, more than technology, practices, or processes alone, can make a difference, whether their business succeeds or fails. Therefore, attracting and retaining top-level talent always ranks high on the list of priorities for executives. In the post-pandemic era, retaining talent has become even more critical. Half of U.S. employees admit to actively searching or keeping a watch for a better opportunity than the job they currently have, according to a 2023 Gallup poll[1]. While employees still consider better pay and benefits a top reason for switching employers—most likely linked to rising inflation in recent years—pay alone is insufficient to keep the organization's best employees. Leaders can take several actions to ensure they retain top talent.

Organizations often claim to invest in employee development but fail to follow through. When cost cutting becomes necessary, the company's training and development budget makes for an easy target. This is a mistake. Turnover carries high costs, not just in terms of talent acquisition costs but also losses in productivity. Providing opportunities to grow and learn builds employee engagement, and more engaged employees are less likely to leave the business. Furthermore, providing employees with additional skills or knowledge will further increase their performance, which ultimately can be a competitive advantage for the company.

The COVID-19 pandemic forced many employers to adopt remote work policies for the first time. Employees who had nearly two years to adjust to working from home and avoid the commute into the office had been reluctant to rejoin the traditional workplace and spend five days a week in the office. Workers have made work-life balance one of their top priorities. Over half of workers surveyed said they would not accept a job that would negatively impact their work-life balance.[2] Unfortunately, many executives have slowly realized the importance of flexible work arrangements. Computer maker, Dell, mandated in early 2024 that employees had to return to the office at least three days a week or would not be considered for promotional opportunities and may even be at risk of losing their jobs. Almost half of Dell's workers ignored the mandate, choosing to work remotely over the risk of losing career advancement or future employment[3]. This provides an important lesson for organizational leaders: understand what is important to your employees to recognize that their desires have shifted toward flexibility.

Culture can be a somewhat nebulous term. Everyone in the organization feels the effect of company culture, but most have difficulty defining it or detailing how to create it. Crafting vision and mission statements may come to mind, but culture is more about how organizations treat employees, how employees treat others, and their attitudes toward how work gets done. It begins with onboarding and extends to employees' daily interactions with their leaders. High-performing companies typically have a few common characteristics regarding their culture: aligned goals, transparent communication, ethical work practices, accountability at all levels, and continuous learning. Culture serves as the glue that binds everyone together and the lubricant that keeps the business moving positively. Unsurprisingly, companies with a strong culture have higher employee satisfaction and retention.

Competition for talent will only grow in the coming years. Companies that thrive truly believe their most valuable assets are their people and prove it through actions to attract and retain employees.

Interesting fact: *A purpose-led organization greatly benefits talent recruitment and retention. Thus, it gives employees something they believe in, work toward, and contribute to. This improves employees' well-being and unifies the organization, resulting in a strong return on investment and profit. (Forbes, 2024)*

In today's dynamic and competitive business landscape, retaining top talent has become a paramount concern for organizations across the globe. The quest for employee retention means more than attracting skilled individuals. It means creating an environment where they choose to stay and thrive. Understanding and harnessing "The Three Forces of Employee Retention" permits this challenge to be met head-on. Combining these "Three Forces" produces the accurate ingredient for success. Leaving one of the forces out of the organizational employee retention strategy undeniably contributes to employees looking elsewhere for employment opportunities.

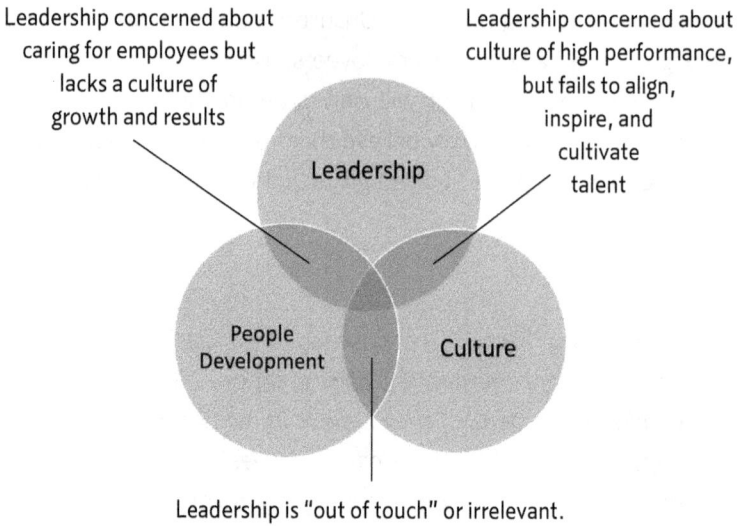

Leadership concerned about caring for employees but lacks a culture of growth and results

Leadership concerned about culture of high performance, but fails to align, inspire, and cultivate talent

Leadership

People Development

Culture

Leadership is "out of touch" or irrelevant.

Figure 2. The Three Forces of Employee Retention

The three forces of employee retention strike a natural alignment between strategic leadership and balancing a high-performance culture with caring for employees' development and personal growth. In some cases, leaders may be so disengaged from the people and daily operations of the business that they become detached and irrelevant.

THE FORCE OF LEADERSHIP

Leadership remains the cornerstone of any successful organization—the driving force that sets the tone, creates a vision, and establishes the overall culture within a company. Effective leaders inspire, motivate, and guide their teams, making employees feel valued and appreciated. Conversely, poor leadership can lead to disengagement, dissatisfaction, and high turnover rates.

The next chapter delves into the pivotal role of leadership in employee retention, exploring how exceptional leaders foster a sense of purpose, provide clear direction, and nurture their employees' growth and development. Real-life examples and practical insights demonstrate how strong leadership can serve as a powerful force in retaining your organization's most valuable assets—its people.

THE FORCE OF CULTURE

Organizational culture is more than just a buzzword; it's the DNA of your company. It encompasses shared values, beliefs, and behaviors that shape the work environment. A positive and supportive culture can make employees feel like they belong and contribute to a sense of loyalty and commitment. Conversely, a toxic or misaligned culture can drive them away.

We will explore the force of culture in employee retention, illustrating how a well-defined culture can attract and retain the right talent while ensuring alignment with the organization's mission and values. We'll also examine strategies to diagnose and transform culture if necessary, and how culture impacts employee engagement, satisfaction, and retention.

THE FORCE OF PEOPLE DEVELOPMENT

No organization operates in isolation; it's a dynamic network of individuals who interact, collaborate, and influence one another. The third force in employee retention focuses on the collective impact of your workforce. It's about fostering positive relationships, teamwork, and a sense of belonging among employees.

For this discussion, we'll explore how the force of developing people within the organization plays a critical role in retaining employees. We'll discuss mentorship and professional growth opportunities and enhancing employee engagement through peer support and collaboration. Through case studies and practical advice, you'll gain insights into how investing in your people can be a potent force in retaining talent.

The following chapters delve deeper into each of these forces, providing actionable strategies and best practices to help you strengthen employee retention in your organization. By understanding and leveraging the force of leadership, culture, and people, you'll be better equipped to create an environment where employees not only want to stay but also thrive, contributing to your business's long-term success and sustainability.

SUMMARY OF CHAPTER 4: THE THREE FORCES OF EMPLOYEE RETENTION

Chapter 4 explores the "Three Forces of Employee Retention," actionable strategies to improve employee engagement, satisfaction, and loyalty, creating an environment where employees choose to stay and thrive, especially in the modern competitive job market.

- **The Force of Leadership** holds that effective leadership is pivotal for employee retention. Strong leaders set the tone for organizational culture, inspire their teams, and provide clear direction while nurturing personal and professional growth to create a positive, retention-friendly environment. Conversely, poor leadership leads to dissatisfaction, disengagement, and high turnover.

- **The Force of Culture**, the DNA of an organization, shapes the shared values, beliefs, and behaviors that typically enjoy higher satisfaction and retention rates, while a toxic or misaligned culture drives talent away. Strategies to diagnose and improve culture are explored, with an emphasis on aligning cultural practices with the organization's mission and values.

- **The Force of People Development** focuses on fostering positive relationships, teamwork, and personal growth opportunities for employees, underscoring the importance of mentorship, professional development, and collaboration. Organizations investing in employee growth and a network of support build a workforce more engaged, motivated, and likely to stay.

By addressing leadership, culture, and people development in tandem, businesses can create an environment where employees not only remain but thrive, contributing to the long-term success of the organization.

KEY BULLET POINTS

- **Three Forces of Employee Retention:**
  - *Leadership*: Inspires, motivates, and guides employees while setting the tone for the organization.
  - *Culture*: Shapes the shared values, beliefs, and behaviors that define the workplace.
  - *People Development*: Promotes growth, teamwork, and positive relationships among employees.

- **Force of Leadership:**
  - Effective leadership fosters purpose, direction, and development.
  - Poor leadership contributes to disengagement and turnover.

- **Force of Culture:**
  - A positive culture enhances belonging and loyalty.
  - Misaligned or toxic cultures drive employees away.

- **Force of People Development:**
  - › Mentorship, collaboration, and growth opportunities strengthen engagement.
  - › Investing in employees creates a motivated and resilient workforce.

- **Holistic Approach:**
  - › Retention strategies must integrate leadership, culture, and people development.
  - › A balanced focus ensures long-term organizational success.

KEY SKILLS AND APPROACHES

- **Leadership Development:**
  - › Cultivate empathy, clear communication, and the ability to inspire purpose.
  - › Provide training for leaders to develop employee-focused management styles.

- **Cultural Alignment:**
  - › Regularly assess and align organizational culture with core values and goals.
  - › Address misaligned or toxic behaviors proactively.

- **Employee Development:**
  - › Design mentorship programs and professional development opportunities.
  - › Encourage collaboration and peer support to foster teamwork.

- **Feedback and Engagement:**
  - › Utilize open communication channels to understand employee needs.

> Create a continuous feedback loop to maintain engagement and trust.

- **Strategic Retention:**
  - > Apply a holistic strategy that balances leadership, culture, and development.
  - > Monitor and adapt retention efforts to evolving workforce dynamics.

QUESTIONS FOR DEEPER UNDERSTANDING

1. How can organizations ensure leaders are equipped to prioritize employee well-being and foster retention?
2. What steps can be taken to diagnose and transform a misaligned organizational culture?
3. How does mentorship contribute to long-term employee retention, and how can it be effectively implemented?
4. What role does employee development play in creating a competitive advantage for organizations?
5. How can organizations balance the needs of diverse generations within a shared culture and development framework?
6. What practical strategies can be used to integrate the three forces of retention into a cohesive strategy?
7. How can organizations measure the effectiveness of leadership, culture, and development initiatives on retention rates?
8. What are the potential risks of focusing too heavily on one of the three forces while neglecting the others?
9. How does the balance of flexibility and structure in organizational culture affect employee satisfaction?
10. What innovations in retention strategies are most likely to be successful in a rapidly changing workforce?

CITATION:

1) www.gallup.com/467702/indicator-employee-retention
-attraction.aspx

2) www.reuters.com/business/
workers-view-work-life-balance-more-important-than-pay
-study-finds-2024-01-17/

3) www.thestreet.com/employment/dell-workers-make-risky
-move-to-dodge-return-to-office-mandate

CHAPTER 5

THE FORCE OF LEADERSHIP

Mickey Hunt Herbert, DBA
Gallagher, Branch President and EVP of Marketing
TOPIC: How Effective Leaders Improve Employee Retention

The rapid evolution of the workforce, driven by the emergence of Generation Y and Generation Z, has necessitated a reevaluation of traditional leadership approaches. These generations bring distinct values, expectations, and aspirations, demanding a shift in leadership styles to engage and retain them effectively. Through a few interviews I conducted and my personal experience managing these generations, here is my assessment of how not to lose a Gen Y or Zer in 10 days!

In an interview with Lacey, a screenwriter, she says, "The biggest two factors that come to mind for me in terms of what would make me stay at a job are room to rise in the ranks and social dynamics/employee curation. I have stayed at jobs that I didn't love and didn't have the best leadership because I loved my coworkers, which, to the boss' credit, was a pool of people curated by their hiring choices. More importantly, the ability to rise and be promoted. I think that as Baby Boomers and Gen X start to move into their retirement phase, some are clinging onto upper-level positions—sometimes to the detriment of the company—and if I get a sense that there will be no opportunity to be promoted in the next 3-5 years, I will start to plan my exit to a job that celebrates retention through earned elevation."

When I interviewed Nathan, a banker, he stated that "all-embracing, transparency, purpose-driven work, and flexibility are commonalities. Gen Y/Z want clear expectations around performance and salary, autonomy to do their jobs their way, and flexibility." He went on to say, "Career growth and compensation are top factors in determining loyalty to a company. Community outreach and diverse senior leadership follows." Effective leadership to Nathan is crucial to employee retention. For example, "You can believe in the company's mission and the work holistically, but if you have an inefficient leader that you report to directly, the system is broken. This comes down to leadership training, accountability, and development across the entire org."

My final interview was with Kyla, a college student. Kyla said she "appreciates leaders that adapt to contemporary values and cultures." For instance, she believes that dedicating your entire life to work is outdated and prioritizes work-like balance, focusing on working to live rather than living to work. Additionally, she said, "Seeking a flexible job doesn't equate to laziness, a misconception often associated with Gen Y and Z."

I summarized through my interviews that Gen Y and Z employees prioritize work-life balance, career purpose, and personal and career growth. They value relationships with employers. Leaders must be authentic, transparent, empathetic, flexible, appreciative, and willing to mentor. When leaders embody these characteristics, they create a positive work environment that aligns with the values and expectations of the generations. If an organization wants to improve employee retention among Gen Y and Z, consider the following recommendations:

1. Invest in leadership programs.
2. Foster open communication and collaboration.
3. Provide growth opportunities and mentorship.
4. Recognize and reward contributions.

5. Embrace work-life balance flexibility.
6. Encourage social responsibility.

By recognizing and addressing each generation's unique needs and expectations, leaders can create a positive work environment that fosters engagement, satisfaction, and commitment.

Interesting fact: *According to LinkedIn, over a quarter of Gen Z and Millennials say the number one reason they'd leave their job is because they did not have the opportunity to learn and grow. But currently, 63% of Millennials said their leadership skills were not being fully developed.*

Effective leadership provides the cornerstone of a thriving organization. This chapter explores how leadership styles directly influence employee retention, and how positive and negative leadership styles shape the employee experience, ultimately determining whether employees choose to stay with the company or leave. Great leaders can navigate the tides of nurturing and developing talent while driving a culture of alignment and results. This balance creates an environment of professional growth and organizational progress that excites people about their work.

Before going further, we must understand the importance and correlation between effective leadership and employee retention. According to a recent Gallup study published by the U.S. Chamber of Commerce, one in two employees have left a position to avoid a bad manager. That is a staggering number. Additionally, LinkedIn platform data (as of late 2023) shows that Gen Z employees in the U.S. are transitioning jobs nearly 40% more than the previous year and more than double the rate of Millennials. A leader asserts massive influence and impact on whether the employee stays or leaves an organization. We have met and discussed this fact with numerous employees across several sectors. In many cases, those employees with highly sought-after skills decide to remain with an organization even with lower pay because of their manager or boss. They can essentially go down the street, do the same job, and make more money; however, they stick around because of their leadership.

This doesn't mean that every time somebody leaves an organization, it is the sole fault of the manager. As we all know, employees leave organizations for various reasons. If an individual works for a leader that they respect and trust, however, the odds of them remaining with the organization certainly increase. Remember the old saying, "The grass is greener on the other side?" The manager's goal is to make the grass *very green* under the employee's feet. Doing so decreases the cost and risk for an employee of going to another organization. If there is no "green grass" under the employee's feet in their current company, then one blade of green grass at another organization justifies the risk of leaving and transitioning. Basically, the employee has nothing to lose in their current situation with an unsatisfactory manager.

We can see this construct of "keeping the grass green" as striking a logical balance between intrinsic and extrinsic motivation. Both motivational constructs are important (Figure 3.) and have their limits. Extrinsic motivation encompasses items like pay and benefits. It can also include company meals, outings, bonuses or good ole' company swag. The motivational impact may be high, but it is short-lived. After just a few months, we quickly forget about the pay raise, bonus, or fancy coffee mug. In addition, employees may even begin to expect the same level of perks year after year. Anything less could feel like a slight.

Intrinsic motivation, on the other hand, directly results from personal or professional growth, meaningful relationships, autonomy, competence, and belonging. Once achieved, employees desire to maintain and expand these factors. Intrinsic motivational factors will typically outweigh the extrinsic ones. This means an employee experiencing mentorship, coaching, and meaningful relationships on the job that contribute to an overall sense of growth and development will stick around even when offered a job with better pay or benefits.

Intrinsic Motivation:	Extrinsic Motivation:
Inherent satisfaction and enjoyment of work based on relationships, interests, and experiences.	Behavior driven by external factors or consequences.
<ul><li>Growth</li><li>Challenge</li><li>Curiosity</li><li>Control</li><li>Purpose</li><li>Enjoyment</li></ul>	<ul><li>Reward</li><li>Punishment</li><li>Power</li><li>Praise</li><li>Competition</li><li>Benefits</li></ul>

Figure 3. Motivation Factors

Organizations will always seek to be competitive with pay, benefits, and external factors within their control to poach the best talent. As a business leader, you cannot always affect this fact. Employment opportunities with better pay and perks always loom out there. With today's technology, organizations can seek out and communicate seamlessly with potential employees to convince them to leave their current organization and accept employment elsewhere. Here's the good news . . . the stronger the intrinsic factors, the harder the decisions for employees to go somewhere else. Great leaders and managers build a strong foundation of motivators that balance what is practical from a pay and benefits standpoint while maximizing the extrinsic motivators at every level. This helps create a solid retention strategy that produces long-term results.

One thing to keep in mind, natural employee attrition cannot be avoided. No matter how good the manager, employees will leave for one reason or another. No magic pill exists for any organization to obtain 100% retention of employees. The goal remains increasing retention as much as possible and reducing the odds of employees seeking employment in another organization.

Furthermore, in today's highly interconnected digital landscape, many technologies exist to facilitate job-seeking and talent acquisition, making it easier than ever for employees to explore alternative opportunities outside their current organizations. Job search platforms such as LinkedIn, Indeed, Ladders, and Glassdoor, provide extensive databases of job openings and networking opportunities, enabling employees to passively or actively seek new roles. Moreover, professional networking sites and social media platforms empower individuals to showcase their skills and expertise to potential employers. At the same time, recruitment software and artificial intelligence algorithms streamline the hiring process for organizations, often targeting passive candidates who may not be actively seeking new opportunities. The ubiquity of these technologies has created a competitive environment where employers must proactively engage and retain their workforce to mitigate the risk of losing valuable talent to external opportunities.

Think about this—in the time someone takes a lunch break, they can apply for dozens of positions! In the same sense, during an employee's workday, they might get dozens of communications for open positions for which they qualify.

When leadership becomes weak, the floodgate opens for employees to take that moment to easily apply for other positions or accept offers from inbound talent acquisition communications.

You might be asking, "This is all great, but how can our leadership foundation be built to the point that employees will think twice before they hand in their resignation letter?" I'm glad you asked—keep reading!

THE ROLE OF POSITIVE LEADERSHIP IN RETENTION

Positive leadership plays a pivotal role in employee retention by fostering a supportive and engaging work environment that cultivates employee loyalty, motivation, and job satisfaction. Positive leaders inspire and empower their team members, providing clear direction, meaningful feedback, and opportunities for growth and development. By demonstrating empathy, trust, and appreciation for their employees' contributions, positive leaders create a sense of belonging and camaraderie that strengthens employee engagement and commitment to the organization. Moreover, positive leadership promotes open communication, transparency, and a culture of recognition, where employees feel valued and respected for their unique talents and perspectives. This fosters a sense of loyalty and attachment to the organization, reducing turnover rates and enhancing employee retention over the long term. Overall, positive leadership drives individual and team performance and contributes to a positive organizational culture that attracts and retains top talent.

Several leadership styles contribute to employee retention, each striking a natural balance between caring for the growth and development of employees and producing a culture that gets results. Here are a few to remember as you progress toward improved employee retention.

TRANSFORMATIONAL LEADERSHIP

Transformational leadership is characterized by leaders who inspire and motivate their followers to achieve extraordinary outcomes and grow personally and professionally. Transformational leaders typically exhibit charisma, vision, intellectual stimulation, and individualized consideration. They inspire and empower their team members to transcend their self-interests and work toward collective goals, fostering a sense of shared purpose and commitment. Transformational leaders challenge the status quo, encourage innovation and creativity, and promote a culture of continuous learning and improvement within the organization.

The impact of transformational leadership on employee retention can be profound. Research has consistently shown that employees who work under transformational leaders tend to exhibit higher levels of engagement, job satisfaction, and organizational commitment, because transformational leaders create a supportive and empowering work environment where employees feel valued, motivated, and invested in the success of the organization. By articulating a compelling vision, providing meaningful feedback and recognition, and fostering open communication and trust, transformational leaders inspire a sense of ownership and accountability among their team members. Moreover, transformational leaders often serve as role models, exemplifying the behaviors and values they expect from their followers, which further strengthens employee engagement and loyalty. Overall, transformational leadership positively impacts employee retention by aligning individual goals with organizational objectives and promoting a culture of high performance and excellence.

Spotlight—Transformational Leader: Winston Churchill

British Prime Minister Winston Churchill's leadership during World War II exemplifies transformational leadership at its core. Taking office in 1940 during Britain's darkest hour, he inspired a nation facing imminent collapse. Churchill led Britain to victory through compelling vision, unwavering resilience, and bold decision-making. His leadership provides valuable lessons for today's business executives, navigating uncertainty and disruption.

Churchill's ability to communicate a clear and motivating vision was crucial. His speeches, including "We shall fight on the beaches...we shall never surrender," turned despair into determination. Business leaders today can learn from his ability to rally teams around a common purpose, fostering trust and commitment in challenging times. Resilience defined Churchill's leadership. He refused to surrender, adapting strategies to overcome near-impossible odds. This mirrors the perseverance needed by modern leaders to navigate economic downturns, technological disruptions, and industry shifts. Leaders who remain steadfast and solution-focused can guide their organizations through adversity.

Churchill also empowered those around him, surrounding himself with top strategists, pressing them for ideas, arriving at a clear course of action, and then trusting them to execute those critical decisions. Today's leaders must do the same—cultivating a culture of trust and collaboration to drive innovation.

Finally, Churchill embraced innovation, championing technological advancements that helped win the war. In business, leaders who adopt forward-thinking strategies and leverage emerging technologies position their organizations for long-term success.

Churchill's principles—vision, resilience, empowerment, and innovation—remain vital for modern leaders. His transformational leadership continues to provide a proven blueprint for navigating uncertainty and building strong, adaptable organizations.

PARTICIPATIVE LEADERSHIP

In participative leadership, also known as democratic leadership, leaders involve employees in decision-making processes, encourage open communication, and value their input and contributions. In a participative leadership approach, leaders seek input from their team members, consider their opinions and ideas, and collaborate with them to make decisions that affect the organization. This leadership style emphasizes shared responsibility, empowerment, and teamwork, fostering a culture of engagement within the organization.

Participative leadership has a significant impact on employee retention. By involving employees in decision-making processes and valuing their input, participative leaders create a sense of ownership and investment in the organization among employees. When employees feel that their voices are heard and their opinions matter, they feel a deeper sense of loyalty and commitment to the organization. Moreover, participative leadership fosters a positive work environment characterized by trust, transparency, and mutual respect, which enhances job satisfaction and employee morale. Employees are more likely to remain with an organization where they feel valued, respected, and empowered to contribute to decision-making. Participative leadership promotes employee retention by creating a culture of collaboration, engagement, and shared accountability.

Spotlight—Participative Leader: Richard Branson

Richard Branson's leadership style is synonymous with collaboration and empowerment, making him a quintessential example of a participative leader.

At the heart of Branson's approach lies a deep-seated belief in the power of people and the importance of fostering a culture of openness and teamwork. Known for his willingness to involve employees at all levels of the organization in decision-making processes, seeking their input, feedback, and ideas, Branson values diversity of thought and encourages individuals to speak up, share their perspectives, and contribute to the company's collective success.

Branson's participative leadership style becomes evident in his hands-on approach to management, as he actively engages with employees, solicits their opinions, and collaborates with them to solve problems and drive innovation. He empowers his teams to take ownership of their work, experiment with new ideas, and pursue creative solutions, fostering a sense of ownership and accountability among employees. By championing participative leadership, Branson has created a culture of trust, respect, and collaboration within his organizations, enabling them to thrive in an ever-changing business landscape.

In essence, Richard Branson's commitment to participative leadership has propelled his companies to success and inspired countless leaders to embrace a more collaborative approach to leadership.

SERVANT LEADERSHIP

Servant leadership defines a leadership philosophy and style characterized by a focus on serving others, prioritizing the needs of employees, and fostering their growth and development. Servant leaders emphasize empathy, humility, and a commitment to serving the greater good of the organization and its stakeholders. Rather than seeking personal power or prestige, servant leaders aim to empower and support their team members, enabling them to reach their full potential and achieve organizational goals. Servant leaders typically demonstrate active listening, empathy, and a willingness to collaborate with their team members to address their needs and concerns.

The impact of servant leadership on employee retention can be significant. By prioritizing the well-being and development of employees, servant leaders create a positive and supportive work environment where employees feel valued, respected, and appreciated. Employees more likely remain with an organization where they feel their contributions are recognized, and their voices heard. Servant leaders also foster a culture of trust, transparency, and open communication, which enhances employee engagement and morale. Moreover, servant leaders empower employees to take ownership of their work and contribute to the organization's success, leading to higher levels of job satisfaction and commitment. Servant leadership promotes employee retention by creating a culture of care, collaboration, and mutual respect within the organization.

Spotlight—Servant Leader: Susan Wojcicki

Susan Wojcicki's tenure as CEO of YouTube exemplifies the essence of servant leadership, where leaders prioritize the needs of others, empower their teams, and work tirelessly to foster growth and development.

Throughout her career, Wojcicki has demonstrated a deep commitment to serving both her employees and the broader community, embodying the values of humility, empathy, and compassion. As CEO of YouTube, Wojcicki prioritized creating a supportive work environment where employees felt valued, respected, and empowered to unleash their full potential. She actively sought out feedback from employees and listened to their concerns.

Wojcicki's servant leadership style was also evident in her focus on serving YouTube's users and content creators, recognizing the platform's impact on society and the responsibility that comes with it. She prioritized transparency, accountability, and user safety, working to address issues such as misinformation, harmful content, and copyright infringement to create a safer and more positive online community. Through her servant leadership approach, Susan Wojcicki has not only achieved remarkable success in her career but has also inspired countless others to embrace servant leadership principles and positively impact their own organizations and communities. Her legacy serves as a powerful reminder of the transformative power of leadership that prioritizes the needs of others above all else.

At the time of this publication, it was sad to hear that Ms. Wojcicki passed away.

"She helped turn Google into an internet juggernaut and became one of the most prominent women in Silicon Valley."
—New York Times, August 2024

It becomes important to understand each of these leadership styles. One style might feel intuitive to you, while others may seem more difficult or require more energy. Knowing these styles enables leaders to adapt as the situation demands. For example, leveraging a transformational style can be helpful when casting a new vision or strategy. Participative leaders thrive in problem-solving and getting the best ideas out of the group. Servant leaders can dramatically impact the organization's day-to-day culture and how people feel about their work. The magic comes in knowing what style to leverage based on the situation.

THE IMPACT OF NEGATIVE LEADERSHIP ON RETENTION

Toxic leadership within organizations poses a significant threat to the retention of Gen Y and Z employees, who remain particularly sensitive to workplace culture, values, and leadership behaviors. Toxic leadership refers to a style of leadership characterized by abusive, manipulative, and destructive behaviors that undermine trust, morale, and well-being within the organization. Leaders who exhibit toxic behaviors often prioritize their own interests over those of their employees, create a culture of fear and intimidation, and fail to foster a supportive work environment. The impact of toxic leadership on the overall organization can be profound, leading to decreased employee morale, engagement, and productivity, as well as higher turnover rates and reputational damage.

One of the most significant consequences of toxic leadership can be seen in its detrimental effect on employee retention, particularly among Gen Y and Z employees. These younger generations are less tolerant of toxic behaviors and more likely to seek employment elsewhere if they feel undervalued, unsupported, or mistreated by their leaders. Toxic leadership erodes trust and confidence in leadership, leading to disengagement, disillusionment, and attrition. Employees who experience toxic leadership may feel demoralized, stressed, and burnt out, leading to decreased job satisfaction and a desire to leave the organization for a healthier work environment.

In addition to impacting employee retention, toxic leadership has broader implications for organizational performance and culture. Toxic leaders often prioritize short-term gains over long-term sustainability, leading to unethical decision-making, poor communication, and a lack of accountability within the organization. This can result in decreased innovation, collaboration, and employee engagement, along with increased turnover, absenteeism, and legal liabilities. Moreover, toxic leadership can damage the organization's reputation, brand image, and ability to attract and retain top talent, leading to long-term financial and reputational consequences.

Toxic leadership poses a significant threat to the retention of Gen Y and Z employees, with far-reaching consequences for organizational performance and culture. Leaders must recognize the damaging impact of toxic behaviors and prioritize creating a positive, inclusive, and supportive work environment that fosters trust, respect, and collaboration. By addressing toxic leadership and promoting ethical, compassionate, and accountable leadership practices, organizations can create a healthier, more sustainable workplace that attracts and retains top talent in today's competitive job market.

THE FIVE LEADERSHIP STRATEGIES TO RETAIN THE MODERN GENERATIONS

STRATEGY #1: BE AN EXPERT AT WHAT GENERATION Y AND Z EMPLOYEES REALLY WANT

The retention of Gen Y and Z employees hinges on managers' ability to understand and adapt to the unique expectations of these generations, even if they themselves are not part of them. Managers must recognize what motivates and engages Gen Y and Z employees, which may differ from traditional leadership approaches or personal beliefs. This requires a willingness to be flexible with their leadership style and embrace change, even if it challenges their perceptions or previous successful strategies. By adapting their leadership approach to align with the expectations of Gen Y and Z, managers can create an environment where these employees feel valued, empowered, and motivated to stay and contribute to the organization's success.

Additionally, modern managers must move beyond the stereotypes and negative perceptions surrounding Gen Y and Z employees. While there may be prevalent myths and misconceptions about these generations, managers must recognize these may not always be accurate or representative of the entire cohort. Instead of relying on hearsay or outdated assumptions, managers should seek to understand the unique characteristics, preferences, and strengths of Gen Y and Z employees within their specific context. By adopting an open-minded and inclusive approach, managers can cultivate positive relationships and create an environment where all employees, regardless of their generation, feel valued, respected, and motivated to contribute their best. Focusing on individual strengths, talents, and potential remains crucial, rather than relying on broad generalizations that may perpetuate unfounded biases and hinder effective leadership and team dynamics.

To put this strategy in basic terms—know employees, know what they want, what they desire, what motivates them, and how they think! "Old school" leadership techniques have been proven outdated and unworkable. As a heart surgeon knows the heart inside and out, a manager should understand their employees at the same level. Only then can the manager effectively adjust leadership strategies to accommodate and retain these complex but valuable generations.

STRATEGY #2: PROVIDE CLEAR EXPECTATIONS

Leaders must provide clear and concise expectations regarding their roles, responsibilities, and performance standards to effectively retain Gen Y and Z employees. Clear expectations set the foundation for mutual understanding between leaders and employees, reducing confusion and ambiguity while promoting accountability and alignment with organizational goals. Several key strategies for leaders to communicate clear expectations to retain Gen Y and Z employees are listed below:

Leaders should clearly outline the specific duties, tasks, and responsibilities associated with each employee's role. This includes defining the scope of their work, key deliverables, and performance metrics.

Providing a detailed job description and discussing expectations during the onboarding process helps Gen Y and Z employees understand what is required of them from the outset.

Individual goal setting is an important part of this process. Leaders should collaborate with Gen Y and Z employees to establish SMART (Specific, Measurable, Achievable, Relevant, Time-bound) performance goals aligning with organizational objectives.

Overall, SMART goals provide a structured approach to goal setting that resonates with Gen Y and Z workers' preferences and values. By setting specific, measurable, achievable, relevant, and time-bound goals, organizations can support the success and development of these employees, leading to higher levels of engagement, satisfaction, and retention.

Understanding SMART Goals

SMART goals provide a framework for setting Specific, Measurable, Achievable, Relevant, and Time-bound objectives. Here's a breakdown of each component:

1. **Specific:** Goals should be clear, well-defined, and specific in what needs to be accomplished. They should answer the questions of who, what, where, when, why, and how.

2. **Measurable:** Goals should include criteria for measuring progress and success. This involves identifying specific metrics or indicators that can be used to track performance and determine whether the goal has been achieved.

3. **Achievable:** Goals should be realistic and attainable within the available resources, constraints, and timeframe. While it's important for goals to be ambitious, they should also be within reach with effort and commitment.

4. **Relevant:** Goals should be relevant and aligned with the overall objectives and priorities of the individual, team, or organization. They should contribute to larger strategic goals and address key areas of focus.

5. **Time-bound:** Goals should have a defined timeframe or deadline for completion. This helps create a sense of urgency and accountability, motivating individuals

to act and progress toward achieving the goal within the specified timeframe.

Why are SMART Goals so important?
SMART goals are particularly important for Gen Y and Z workers due to several reasons:

1. **Clarity and Direction:** Gen Y and Z employees value clarity and direction in their work. SMART goals provide clear and specific objectives, helping these employees understand what is expected of them and how their efforts contribute to larger organizational goals.

2. **Motivation and Engagement:** Setting achievable and measurable goals can motivate Gen Y and Z workers by providing a sense of purpose and accomplishment. With clearly defined and attainable goals, employees feel more engaged and motivated to work toward achieving them.

3. **Accountability and Responsibility:** SMART goals create a framework for accountability and responsibility. By establishing clear expectations and deadlines, Gen Y and Z workers can be held accountable for their performance and results.

4. **Professional Development:** SMART goals can support the professional development and growth of Gen Y and Z employees. By setting relevant goals that align with their career aspirations, employees can focus on acquiring new skills, gaining experience, and advancing in their careers.

5. **Feedback and Progress Tracking:** SMART goals provide a basis for ongoing feedback and progress tracking. Managers can regularly review progress toward goals, provide feedback on performance, and adjust as needed to ensure that employees stay on track to achieve their objectives.

By setting SMART goals, individuals and teams can increase clarity, focus, and accountability, leading to greater effectiveness and success in achieving desired outcomes.

Clearly defining performance expectations helps employees understand what success looks like and provides a roadmap for achieving their goals. Regularly reviewing and revising performance goals ensures ongoing clarity and alignment.

STRATEGY #3: OFFER OPEN COMMUNICATION AND CONTINUAL FEEDBACK

Open communication and continual feedback serve as essential elements in retaining Gen Y and Z employees in the workplace. These younger generations value transparency, collaboration, and ongoing dialogue with their managers and peers. Organizations can effectively engage and retain Gen Y and Z talent by fostering an environment where communication channels remain open and feedback encouraged.

Open communication cultivates trust and transparency within the workplace, critical for building strong relationships between managers and employees. When communication channels are open, Gen Y and Gen Z employees feel empowered to express their ideas, concerns, and feedback without fear of judgment or reprisal, making them feel valued and respected for their contributions.

Furthermore, continual feedback provides Gen Y and Z employees with the guidance and support they need to succeed in their roles. Regular feedback sessions allow managers to recognize employees' achievements, provide constructive criticism, and offer guidance on areas for improvement. This ongoing feedback loop helps employees understand how their work aligns with organizational goals, clarifies expectations, and promotes a culture of continuous learning and development.

By prioritizing open communication and continual feedback, organizations demonstrate their commitment to supporting their Gen Y and Z employees' growth and success. This proactive approach to communication fosters stronger relationships, enhances employee engagement, and ultimately increases retention rates. When employees feel heard, valued, and supported, they are likelier to remain loyal to their organization and invest in their long-term career development. Open communication and continual feedback provide powerful tools for retaining Gen Y and Z employees, driving organizational success and sustainability in today's competitive workforce landscape.

Additionally, Gen Y and Z employees display curiosity and inquisitiveness, often asking the question "Why?" in various contexts. This inclination toward seeking deeper understanding stems from several factors intrinsic to these generations' upbringing and societal influences. First, Gen Y and Z individuals have grown up in an era of rapid technological advancement and instant access to information. With the internet and smartphones at their fingertips, they are accustomed to finding answers quickly and easily. This instant gratification culture has cultivated a desire for immediate knowledge and understanding.

Moreover, these generations have been raised in an environment that values individualism, critical thinking, and self-expression. They are taught to question the status quo, challenge assumptions, and seek rationale behind decisions and actions. Asking "Why?" is a natural extension of this mindset, as they strive to make informed decisions and understand the underlying reasons behind policies, procedures, and directives.

It's essential for managers to recognize that by asking "Why?" Gen Y and Z employees are not challenging authority or questioning intelligence. Rather, they seek clarification, context, and justification to make sense of their work environment and tasks. By understanding this motivation behind the questioning, managers can foster open communication and transparency, addressing concerns and providing meaningful explanations that resonate with these employees.

Similarly, the desire for continuous feedback and performance evaluation stems from Gen Y and Gen Z employees' inclination towards self-improvement and personal development. Having grown up in an era of instant feedback through social media likes, comments, and shares, they expect timely and constructive feedback in the workplace as well. This feedback loop allows them to gauge their progress, identify areas for improvement, and take proactive steps to enhance their performance.

The tendency of Gen Y and Z employees to ask "Why?" and seek frequent feedback reflects their curiosity, desire for understanding, and penchant for continuous improvement. Managers should embrace this mindset by fostering a culture of open communication, transparency, and feedback, ultimately leading to greater engagement, satisfaction, and retention among these employees.

STRATEGY #4: RECOGNIZE AND APPRECIATE CONTRIBUTIONS

Recognizing and appreciating the work of Gen Y and Z employees is crucial for retaining talent in today's workforce. These younger generations place a high value on feeling valued, respected, and appreciated for their contributions. Here's why managers need to recognize and appreciate the work of Gen Y and Z employees and why these generations demand it from their managers:

1. **Validation of Efforts:** Gen Y and Z employees seek validation and recognition for their efforts and achievements. They want to know that their work makes a meaningful impact and contributes to the organization's success. Recognition from managers reinforces their sense of value and motivates them to continue performing at their best.

2. **Boost to Morale and Motivation:** Their managers' recognition and appreciation boost the morale and motivation of Gen Y and Z employees, reinforcing positive behaviors, increasing job satisfaction, and fostering a sense of loyalty. Employees who feel appreciated remain engaged, productive, and committed to their work.

3. **Retention and Loyalty:** Recognition and appreciation play a significant role in employee retention. Gen Y and Z employees are more likely to stay with organizations where their contributions are acknowledged and appreciated. By recognizing and appreciating their work, managers can increase employee loyalty and reduce turnover rates, saving the organization time and resources for recruitment and training.

4. **Fulfillment of Expectations:** In today's interconnected world, Gen Y and Z employees expect instant feedback and recognition through

social media and digital platforms, as well as similar levels of appreciation in the workplace. Failing to recognize their efforts can lead to disengagement and dissatisfaction among these employees.

5. **Fostering a Positive Work Culture:** Recognition and appreciation foster a positive work culture where employees feel valued, supported, and respected. This positive work environment improves employee morale and motivation and enhances collaboration, teamwork, and overall organizational performance.

Managers must recognize and appreciate the work of Gen Y and Z employees to retain talent and foster a positive work environment. By acknowledging their contributions, managers can increase employee morale, motivation, and loyalty, ultimately leading to higher levels of engagement, productivity, and retention within the organization. Failure to recognize and appreciate these employees' efforts can harm employee satisfaction, retention, and organizational success.

STRATEGY #5: BE A COACH VS. A MANAGER

In today's rapidly evolving workplace landscape, the traditional commanding leadership style continues to become increasingly outdated, particularly when it comes to managing Gen Y and Z employees. These younger generations value autonomy, collaboration, and personal development, making a coach-like leadership approach essential for retaining talent. Here's why managers need to be coaches to Gen Y and Z employees and why these generations demand this from their managers:

1. **Support for Growth and Development:** Gen Y and Z employees prioritize learning, growth, and

skill development opportunities. They expect their managers to act as mentors and guides, providing support, feedback, and resources to help them reach their full potential. A coach-like leadership approach encourages continuous learning and empowers employees to take ownership of their personal and professional development.

2. **Focus on Collaboration and Partnership:** Unlike the hierarchical model, a coach-like leadership style emphasizes collaboration and partnership between managers and their employees. Managers serve as facilitators, working alongside team members to set goals, solve problems, and achieve shared objectives. This collaborative approach fosters trust, communication, and teamwork, leading to higher levels of engagement and productivity.

3. **Adaptability and Flexibility:** Gen Y and Z employees thrive in adaptable and flexible environments. They value leaders open to new ideas, receptive to feedback, and willing to adapt their approach based on individual needs and preferences. A coach-like leadership style encourages flexibility and agility, allowing managers to tailor their coaching methods to meet the unique needs of each employee.

4. **Empowerment and Autonomy:** A coach-like leadership approach empowers Gen Y and Z employees to take ownership of their work and make decisions autonomously. Instead of micromanaging or dictating tasks, managers provide guidance, support, and resources, allowing employees to explore creative

solutions, take calculated risks, and learn from their experiences. This sense of autonomy fosters a culture of innovation, initiative, and accountability within the organization.

5. **Enhanced Engagement and Retention:** By adopting a coach-like leadership style, managers can increase employee engagement and retention among Gen Y and Gen Z employees. Coaching promotes a sense of purpose, fulfillment, and career progression, leading to greater job satisfaction and loyalty to the organization. Employees tend to stay with companies where they feel supported, challenged, and valued by their managers.

The shift toward a coach-like leadership style is essential for retaining talent in today's workforce, particularly among Gen Y and Z employees. By prioritizing growth, collaboration, adaptability, empowerment, and engagement, managers can create a positive and supportive work environment that attracts and retains top talent, ultimately driving organizational success in the long run.

Self-Assessment: A leader's personal reflection on past performance or conversations with direct reports is vital. It may seem obvious, but leaders seeking to be the best regularly reflect on their actions, determine what they would do differently next time, apply a new practice, and assess the result. In addition, the best leaders are constantly seeking additional sources of feedback to improve.

Managers should regularly engage in self-assessment for several important reasons:

1. **Continuous Improvement:** Self-assessment allows managers to identify areas of strength and areas for improvement in their leadership practices. By reflecting on their performance, managers can develop strategies to enhance their effectiveness and become better leaders over time.

2. **Personal Growth:** Self-assessment allows managers to gain insights into their strengths, weaknesses, and areas of development. This self-awareness enables them to set goals for personal growth and take proactive steps to enhance their skills and capabilities.

3. **Enhanced Leadership Skills:** Managers can identify gaps in their leadership skills and knowledge through self-assessment. By addressing these gaps, managers can strengthen their leadership abilities, such as communication, decision-making, conflict resolution, and team building, leading to improved performance and results.

4. **Better Decision-Making:** Self-assessment helps managers become more objective and analytical in their decision-making processes. By evaluating their actions and outcomes, managers can learn from past experiences and make more informed decisions in the future.

5. **Increased Employee Engagement:** Managers who engage in self-assessment demonstrate a commitment to personal and professional growth, which can inspire their team members to do the same. This can foster a culture of continuous improvement and learning within the organization, leading to higher levels of employee engagement and satisfaction.

6. **Accountability:** Self-assessment encourages managers to take ownership of their actions and outcomes. By holding themselves accountable for their performance, managers set a positive example for their team members and create a culture of accountability within the organization.

Overall, self-assessment offers a valuable tool for managers to enhance their leadership skills, drive personal and professional growth, and contribute to the success of their teams and organizations. By regularly evaluating their performance and seeking opportunities for improvement, managers can become more effective leaders and achieve greater success in their roles.

Now that you understand more about the leadership strategies for retaining Gen Y and Z, it is time for your Self-Assessment. Look at the following assessment chart. How would you honestly rate yourself? If you find that you need some work in any given area, that's OK! The point is not to be "perfect" but to be willing to learn, change, and adapt to the complexity of what employees demand of managers and leaders. Embrace the journey—and continue to work on your own skillset, which will inevitably be appreciated by your employees.

LEADERSHIP STRATEGY ASSESSMENT

As a leader/manager in your organization, how would you rate yourself?			
Leadership Strategy	**Doing Good**	**Needs Work**	**How can you improve?**
Know what Gen Y/Z Really Want			

Provide Clear Expectations			
Foster Open Communication and Feedback			
Recognize and Appreciate Contributions			
Be a Coach			

Remember, leadership is not a one-size-fits-all endeavor, and its influence on employee retention cannot be understated. Positive leadership styles, such as transformational, participative, and servant leadership, empower and inspire employees to remain committed to their organizations. Conversely, negative leadership can drive employees away.

The key takeaway? Leadership matters—a lot. Organizations prioritizing developing positive leadership strategies and fostering a supportive, empowering, and constructive environment have proven to be more likely to retain their most valuable asset: their employees. In the end, the impact of leadership on retention moves far beyond just an academic concept; it represents a reality that shapes the destiny of businesses and the livelihoods of countless individuals.

SUMMARY OF CHAPTER 5: THE FORCE OF LEADERSHIP

Chapter 5 underscores the profound impact leadership has on employee retention, emphasizing the role of effective leadership styles in aligning with the expectations of Gen Y and Gen Z employees. These younger generations prioritize flexibility, transparency, mentorship, work-life balance, and opportunities for growth. The chapter integrates insights from interviews and research to explore how positive leadership retains talent, while poor leadership accelerates turnover.

Effective leaders build environments where employees feel valued, challenged, and connected to a shared purpose. Leadership styles such as transformational, participative, and servant leadership are highlighted as pivotal for fostering intrinsic motivation, employee engagement, and loyalty. Transformational leaders inspire innovation and growth, participative leaders encourage collaboration and shared decision-making, and servant leaders prioritize the well-being and development of their teams. These styles not only enhance individual satisfaction but also strengthen organizational performance.

The chapter also probes the negative effects of toxic leadership, which can erode morale, trust, and engagement. Gen Y and Gen Z employees, in particular, remain highly sensitive to leadership behaviors and have proven more likely to leave organizations with weak or damaging leaders. This reality underscores the importance of leadership accountability and the need for continuous improvement in leadership practices.

Practical strategies for retaining employees include understanding what motivates Gen Y and Z, providing clear expectations, fostering open communication, recognizing contributions, and adopting a coaching mindset. Leaders must adapt their approaches to meet the unique needs of their workforce, balancing intrinsic motivators like purpose and growth with extrinsic factors like compensation and benefits.

The chapter emphasizes the value of self-assessment and reflection in leadership, encouraging leaders to continuously refine their skills. It also warns of the competitive job market enabled by technology, where employees can easily explore other opportunities if their current environment falls short.

Ultimately, the chapter asserts that effective leadership is foundational to retention. By creating a supportive, empowering culture, leaders can retain top talent, reduce turnover costs, and drive long-term organizational success.

KEY BULLET POINTS

- **Leadership's Role in Retention:** Strong leadership directly impacts employee loyalty and turnover rates.

- **Generational Expectations:** Gen Y and Z value transparency, growth opportunities, and work-life balance.

- **Positive Leadership Styles:**
  - *Transformational*: Inspires innovation and aligns employees with organizational vision.
  - *Participative*: Encourages collaboration and shared decision-making.
  - *Servant*: Prioritizes employee well-being and development.

- **Negative Leadership:** Toxic behaviors erode trust, morale, and engagement, leading to higher turnover.

- **Practical Strategies:**
  - › Understand employee needs and motivations.
  - › Provide clear expectations and SMART goals.
  - › Foster open communication and continual feedback.
  - › Recognize and appreciate contributions.
  - › Embrace a coaching mindset over a commanding style.

- **Self-Assessment:** Leaders must reflect on and improve their effectiveness to meet evolving employee demands.

- **Job Market Dynamics:** Technology facilitates easy job-seeking, increasing the need for strong leadership retention strategies.

KEY SKILLS AND APPROACHES

- **Adaptability:** Tailor leadership styles to meet the unique needs of employees and situations.
- **Emotional Intelligence:** Demonstrate empathy, active listening, and authentic appreciation for team members.
- **Communication:** Foster open channels for dialogue, feedback, and transparency.
- **Coaching Mindset:** Act as a mentor to guide employees toward personal and professional growth.
- **Recognition Practices:** Regularly acknowledge and celebrate individual and team achievements.
- **Visionary Thinking:** Align employees with a compelling organizational mission.
- **Self-Reflection:** Engage in regular assessments to identify areas for leadership improvement.

QUESTIONS FOR DEEPER UNDERSTANDING

1. What are the most effective ways to balance intrinsic and extrinsic motivators for employee retention?
2. How can leaders transition from a commanding style to a coaching mindset effectively?
3. What steps can organizations take to identify and mitigate toxic leadership behaviors?
4. How can self-assessment tools help leaders adapt to generational expectations?
5. What specific actions can leaders take to foster a culture of open communication and feedback?
6. How do transformational, participative, and servant leadership styles complement each other in practice?
7. What are the long-term organizational benefits of prioritizing leadership development?
8. How can technology be leveraged to enhance leadership effectiveness and employee engagement?
9. What role does recognition play in shaping employee loyalty, and how can it be optimized?
10. How can leaders proactively address generational stereotypes to build trust and inclusivity?

CHAPTER 6

THE FORCE
OF CULTURE

Hannah Godfrey
Performance Review Institute, London, England, Vice
President, Professional Development
TOPIC: How Positive Organizational Culture Improves
Employee Retention

Company culture is all pervasive but cannot be seen. It influences every aspect of an organization but cannot be bought. Instead, culture must be established, then nurtured and protected at every level of the company but crucially by its leaders. Financial success and significantly a company's ability to retain its employees, particularly the younger generations, are direct consequences of a positive culture.

As a leader born on the cusp of Generation Y and with a sixteen-year tenure in my current organization, culture is crucial to my loyalty. Unequivocal support through changing times in my personal life, trust fostered through relationships with my peers and my leaders, and ultimately being trusted to lead others changed my professional life forever. The culture of my organization created opportunity. Had I not been challenged, supported, and empowered, I would have undoubtedly moved on. A positive culture is fundamental to creating an environment in which young employees and future leaders can thrive and feel confident they are part of an organization invested in their future.

Today, I lead a diverse international team of a mix of generations. Each member has individual strengths and vulnerabilities, personal hopes, and professional goals. I consider it my responsibility to uphold a culture in which those aspirations, however small or large, can be fulfilled, and I do this by listening. Dedicating one-to-one time with each of my direct reports is a priority and my conduit to truly understanding how to motivate, support, and guide them. It's also an expectation I set for my managers with their direct reports. If you're not talking to your team, how do you help? How do you sustain that all-important positive culture?

Through these regular meetings with the Gen Z members of my team, I sense a real desire to contribute to society and the increasing importance they place on broader societal issues like sustainability and inclusion. Any company that ignores these modern workforce issues creates a barrier between itself and the next generation of employees. Young people have the freedom to choose where they begin their careers and exercise that choice without fear. They gravitate toward progressive, open-minded companies that truly value their employees as individuals.

Interesting fact: *According to Harvard University, it's estimated that the average adult living in the United States will spend 90,000 hours—or one-third of their lives—at work. That's a significant amount of time—why not spend it somewhere that is enjoyable, motivating, and inspiring?*

Organizational culture is the heartbeat of any company. In this chapter, we explore how organizational culture directly affects employee retention, examining the ways positive and negative cultures shape the employee experience, ultimately determining whether employees choose to stay with the company.

WHY IS ORGANIZATIONAL CULTURE SO IMPORTANT?

Organizational culture serves as the bedrock of any successful enterprise, shaping the values, behaviors, and experiences of employees at every level of the organization. A positive and inclusive culture fosters engagement, drives performance, and enhances employee satisfaction, while a toxic or dysfunctional culture can have detrimental effects on morale, productivity, and retention. Recent research conducted by the Society for Human Resource Management (SHRM) sheds light on the profound impact of organizational culture on employee attitudes and behaviors:

- Most workers who contemplate leaving their current employer work for organizations with poor cultures.

- Ninety percent of workers who rate their organizational culture as poor have considered quitting, compared to 72 percent of those who rate it as average and 32 percent of those who rate it as good.

- Nearly one in three workers (32 percent) dread going to work, often due to a poor workplace culture.

- Forty-two percent of workers globally have witnessed inconsiderate or insensitive treatment of a coworker by a manager in the past year.

- Six in ten workers (60 percent) actively searching for a job report that their organization's culture makes it difficult to balance their work and home commitments.

These findings underscore the critical role that organizational culture plays in shaping employee experiences and organizational outcomes.

WHAT IS ORGANIZATIONAL CULTURE?

Organizational culture can be defined as a multifaceted and elusive concept at the core of every workplace, shaping its identity, values, and behaviors. Defined as the shared beliefs, values, norms, and customs that guide the behavior of individuals within an organization, culture often equates to the "personality" or "soul" of a company. However, capturing the essence of culture is no easy feat, as it can be perceived differently by each person and often manifests as a subtle yet palpable feeling that employees experience in their day-to-day interactions.

While some may thrive in a particular culture, others may find it stifling or uncomfortable, highlighting the subjective nature of cultural perceptions. Nonetheless, organizations with strong cultures share common characteristics, such as clear values, a sense of belonging, and a collective sense of purpose, which foster cohesion, engagement, and commitment among employees. Conversely, negative cultures characterized by toxicity, distrust, and disengagement can have detrimental effects on employee morale, productivity, and retention.

Recognizing the critical role that culture plays in shaping organizational dynamics, leaders must take deliberate steps to build and maintain a culture that aligns with the organization's values and objectives. By cultivating a culture of trust, respect, and authenticity, leaders can create an environment where employees feel valued, motivated, and empowered to contribute their best work. In this chapter, we explore the importance of organizational culture, its impact on employee retention, and strategies for cultivating a positive and sustainable culture that drives organizational success.

EXPLAINING HOW CULTURE IMPACTS EMPLOYEE RETENTION

Interesting Fact: *Over the past five years, the cost of turnover due to workplace culture exceeded $223 billion. (SHRM, 2024)*

Navigating the vast sea of information on organizational culture and employee retention can be overwhelming, with thousands of pages and alternative perspectives vying for attention. The sheer volume of findings and opinions on the topic can often leave readers feeling confused and uncertain about where to begin. However, amidst the complexity, clarity may be found.

By breaking down the concept of organizational culture into its major components, we can gain a deeper understanding of its impact on employee retention and identify actionable strategies for improvement. These components serve as pillars upon which organizations can build a culture that fosters engagement, satisfaction, and loyalty among employees, ultimately contributing to their long-term retention and success within the organization.

THE STRUCTURE OF ORGANIZATIONAL CULTURE

Imagine organizational culture as the blueprint for constructing a sturdy and resilient building, with each component meticulously designed to uphold the structure and support its inhabitants (Figure 4.).

In this chapter, we explore an analogy that conceptualizes organizational culture through the lens of six key components:

Mission, Values, and Motivational Factors, each supported through Leadership, Communication, and Accountability (Figure 4). Just as a building relies on its pillars to provide strength and stability, organizations depend on their cultural pillars to foster an environment conducive to employee retention.

The foundation, pillars, and gables serve as the cornerstones of positive and cohesive culture, intertwining to create a robust framework that enhances employee engagement, satisfaction, and loyalty. By examining each pillar in-depth and understanding its specific components, we can gain valuable insights into how organizational culture influences employee retention and identify actionable strategies for strengthening each pillar to support long-term success. Through this creative exploration, we will uncover the key principles and practices that underpin a thriving organizational culture and pave the way for enhanced employee retention.

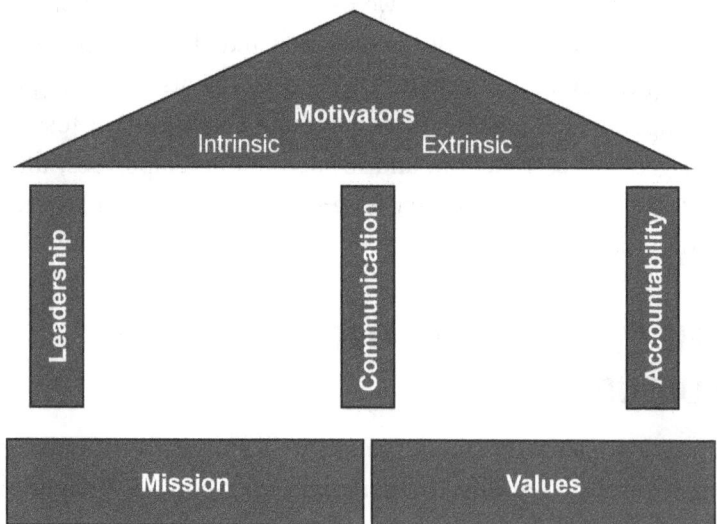

Figure 4. The Structure of Organizational Culture

THE FOUNDATION

The first and most crucial component of the cultural structure can be found in the foundation, or the organization's mission and values. The mission provides a sense of true purpose that unifies your team. Core values, on the other hand, serve as the guiding principles that shape the behavior, decision-making, and overall ethos of the organization. In this chapter, we delve into how mission and values intertwine to form the foundation of a strong and enduring organizational culture.

Mission

The concept of a unified purpose emerges as a compelling force in retaining Gen Y and Z employees. These younger cohorts seek more than just a paycheck or job title—they yearn for a sense of belonging and alignment with an organization's mission, values, and ethical standards. When employees feel a unified purpose resonating with their own beliefs and aspirations, they can better develop a deep sense of commitment and loyalty to the organization, increasing retention and driving long-term success.

A unified purpose within an organization goes beyond mere profitability or market share—it encapsulates a shared vision that inspires and unites employees across all levels and departments. For example, Patagonia, an outdoor clothing company, has a clear and compelling purpose to "build the best product, cause no unnecessary harm, and use business to inspire and implement solutions to the environmental crisis." This unified purpose not only guides the company's product development and operations, but also serves as a rallying cry for employees passionate about environmental sustainability.

Similarly, TOMS, a footwear and apparel company, operates under the ethos of "One for One," where for every product sold, a new item gets donated to a person in need. This unified purpose of social impact resonates deeply with Gen Y and Z employees, who prioritize corporate social responsibility and giving back to the community. As a result, TOMS has been able to attract and retain employees aligned with its mission of making a positive difference in the world.

When employees feel that their personal values and ethical standards synch with those of the organization, they experience a sense of fulfillment and purpose in their work. This alignment creates a virtuous cycle where employees not only feel motivated to perform at their best but also harbor a deep sense of pride and ownership in contributing to the organization's mission. For example, employees at Tesla, the electric vehicle manufacturer, remain driven by the company's mission to accelerate the world's transition to sustainable energy. This shared purpose fuels innovation, collaboration, and employee engagement, ultimately leading to higher retention rates and organizational success.

Moreover, organizations with a unified purpose can better attract and retain top talent, particularly among Gen Y and Z employees drawn to meaningful work and social impact. When employees believe in the organization's mission and feel that their work contributes to a larger purpose, they stay loyal and committed, even in the face of challenges or opportunities elsewhere.

The presence of a unified purpose within an organization serves as a powerful driver of employee retention, especially among Gen Y and Z employees who seek purposeful and meaningful work. By aligning the organization's mission, values, and ethical standards with those of its employees, leaders can create a culture of purpose and belonging that inspires loyalty, engagement, and long-term commitment. Examples of companies with clear and compelling purposes prove that organizations prioritizing a unified purpose can better retain top talent and thrive in today's competitive landscape.

Values

In today's rapidly evolving business landscape, the significance of having well-defined core values within an organization cannot be overstated. Core values serve as the fundamental beliefs and guiding principles that dictate behavior, shape the organizational culture, and influence the decision-making processes. They represent the essence of an organization's identity and play a critical role in driving its mission and vision. This section delves into the importance of organizational core values, their composition, benefits, and their profound impact on employee retention. It also explores how the alignment of core values with those of employees, particularly from Gen Y and Z, enhances retention and engagement.

What Are Core Values?

Core values describe the deeply ingrained principles that guide an organization's actions and serve as its cultural cornerstones. They provide the bedrock of an organization's identity, influencing how it conducts business, interacts with stakeholders, and makes strategic decisions. Core values typically encompass a range of elements, including:

1. **Integrity:** Upholding honesty and strong moral principles in all dealings.
2. **Innovation:** Encouraging creativity and continuous improvement.
3. **Respect:** Fostering an environment of mutual respect and consideration.
4. **Excellence:** Striving for superior performance and quality.
5. **Teamwork:** Promoting collaboration and collective effort.
6. **Customer Focus:** Prioritizing customer satisfaction and needs.

Benefits of Core Values

The establishment and adherence to core values yield numerous benefits for organizations. These benefits extend across various dimensions, including organizational performance, employee engagement, and brand reputation. Some of the key benefits include:

1. **Enhanced Decision-Making:** Core values provide a consistent framework for decision-making, ensuring that choices align with the organization's principles and long-term goals.

2. **Strengthened Organizational Identity:** A clear set of core values helps to define the organization's unique identity and differentiate it from competitors.

3. **Improved Employee Engagement:** When employees resonate with the organization's core values, they feel more engaged and motivated.

4. **Increased Trust and Loyalty:** Core values that emphasize integrity and respect build trust among employees, customers, and other stakeholders.

5. **Attraction and Retention of Talent:** Organizations with strong, positive core values attract like-minded individuals and retain top talent.

The Link Between Core Values and Employee Retention

Employee retention poses a critical challenge for many organizations. High turnover rates can lead to increased recruitment and training costs, disrupted workflows, and loss of institutional knowledge. Core values play a pivotal role in fostering employee retention in several ways:

1. **Alignment and Belonging:** Employees who align with an organization's core values are more likely to feel a sense of belonging and purpose. This alignment fosters a positive work environment where employees are committed to the organization's success.

2. **Job Satisfaction:** Core values that promote respect, teamwork, and personal growth contribute to higher job satisfaction. Satisfied employees are less likely to seek opportunities elsewhere.

3. **Cultural Fit:** During the recruitment process, organizations that emphasize their core values can attract candidates who share similar values, enhancing cultural fit and reducing turnover.

4. **Motivation and Engagement:** Core values that emphasize recognition, collaboration, and development motivate employees to perform at their best and remain engaged with their work.

Examples of Core Values in Action
To illustrate the impact of core values on employee retention, consider the following examples:

1. **Google:** Google's core values include a commitment to innovation, user focus, and respect for employees. These values gain reflection in their open and collaborative culture, which attracts and retains top talent.

2. **Patagonia:** Patagonia's core values emphasize environmental responsibility, integrity, and product quality. Employees passionate about sustainability

become drawn to Patagonia, resulting in high levels of retention.

3. **Zappos:** Zappos, known for its customer-centric core values and unique company culture, emphasizes employee happiness and service excellence, leading to strong employee loyalty and low turnover rates.

Generational Perspectives on Core Values

Generations Y and Z have distinct perspectives on work and values compared with previous generations. Understanding their preferences becomes crucial for organizations aiming to attract and retain these cohorts.

Generation Y (Millennials)

- **Value Alignment:** Millennials seek alignment between their personal values and the organization's mission and values. They prioritize organizations that demonstrate social responsibility and ethical behavior.

- **Work-Life Balance:** This generation values work-life balance and prefers organizations that support flexibility and employee well-being.

- **Purpose and Impact:** Millennials feel motivated by a sense of purpose and a desire to make a meaningful impact through their work.

Generation Z

- **Authenticity:** Generation Z values authenticity and transparency. They find themselves attracted to organizations that display honesty about their practices and values.

- **Technological Integration**: As digital natives, they expect organizations to leverage technology effectively and offer opportunities for digital engagement.

The Consequence of Misalignment

When a disconnect exists between an organization's core values and those of its employees, particularly among Gen Y and Z, retention can become a significant issue. Employees who do not see a direct connection between their values and the organization's mission become more likely to seek employment elsewhere. This misalignment can lead to:

1. **Decreased Engagement:** Employees who feel disconnected from the organization's values may exhibit lower levels of engagement and motivation.

2. **Increased Turnover:** Misalignment can result in higher turnover rates as employees look for organizations that better reflect their values and aspirations.

3. **Negative Workplace Culture:** A lack of shared values can contribute to a fragmented and less cohesive workplace culture.

Organizational core values mean more than just statements on a website or in a handbook; they drive a company's culture and success. By clearly defining and living their core values, organizations can create an environment that attracts and retains employees not only skilled but also deeply committed to the organization's mission and vision. This alignment emerges as particularly crucial for engaging and retaining Gen Y and Z, who place a high emphasis on values and purpose in their careers. Ultimately, the careful cultivation and integration of core values lead to a more motivated, engaged, and loyal workforce, driving long-term success and stability for the organization.

PILLARS

The organizational structure is held together by the distinct pillars of leadership, communication, and accountability rooted in the foundation of mission and values while holding up the gables that provide the key to overall employee motivation. These pillars have a direct effect on the integrity of the cultural structure and require continuous focus, learning, and improvement.

Leadership

Effective leadership serves as a cornerstone of any successful organization, profoundly influencing employee retention by fostering a positive organizational culture. As previously identified in this book, leadership stands as one of the three primary forces driving employee retention. It serves as a foundational component of organizational culture, directly contributing to the development and maintenance of an environment that both attracts and retains top talent.

Leadership plays a crucial role in setting the stage for an organization's mission, vision, and core values, the guiding principles that shape the organization's identity and operations. Effective leaders accept responsibility for clearly articulating these principles and deeply embedding them in the organizational culture. By doing so, leaders create a sense of purpose and direction that resonates with employees, fostering a strong sense of alignment and commitment.

The development and maintenance of a positive organizational culture remain integral to retaining employees. Leaders serve as powerful agents in this process, influencing behavior, setting expectations, and modeling the values for which the organization stands. A positive culture, characterized by mutual respect, collaboration, and a shared sense of purpose, plays an essential role in employee satisfaction and engagement. When employees feel valued and aligned with the organization's mission and values, they remain loyal and committed to the organization.

Communicating core values to employees falls to leadership as a critical responsibility. Core values provide the fundamental beliefs that guide an organization's actions and decisions. They provide a consistent framework for behavior and serve as a benchmark for evaluating performance. Effective leaders understand the importance of clearly and consistently communicating these values to all members of the organization. This communication should not be limited to formal settings such as meetings or training sessions but should be integrated into everyday interactions and decision-making processes.

Leaders must live the core values each day. Simply stating these values in a mission statement or handbook does not suffice. Leaders must actively demonstrate them through their actions and decisions. For instance, if integrity is a core value, leaders must consistently show honesty and transparency in their dealings. If teamwork is a core value, leaders should foster a collaborative environment where all employees feel supported and valued. By embodying these values, leaders set a powerful example for others to follow, reinforcing the importance of these principles and embedding them into the organizational culture.

Gen Y and Z bring unique perspectives and expectations to the workplace, particularly regarding the alignment of personal and organizational values. These generations seek meaningful work, highly motivated by purpose and impact. They look for organizations whose mission, vision, and values resonate with their own beliefs and aspirations. Effective leaders recognize this and strive to create an environment where these values get both communicated and visibly practiced.

For Gen Y and Z, respect and trust in leadership remain paramount. They need to believe that their leaders feel genuinely committed to the values they espouse and lead the organization with integrity and vision. When these employees perceive a disconnect between the communicated values and the actual behavior of leaders, it undermines their trust and engagement. This misalignment can lead to decreased motivation and higher turnover, as these employees may likely seek employment elsewhere if they feel that the organization does not manifest its stated values.

Conversely, when employees see a direct connection between their values and those of the organization, retention rates improve. Effective leaders who consistently communicate and embody the organization's core values create a sense of alignment and belonging among employees. This alignment fosters a positive work environment where employees feel valued and motivated to contribute to the organization's success. It also enhances job satisfaction, as employees become more engaged and committed when they see their personal values reflected in their work.

Effective leadership also involves creating opportunities for employees to engage with and contribute to the organization's mission and vision. This can be achieved through regular communication, involving employees in decision-making processes, and recognizing their contributions. Leaders should foster an environment where employees feel their voices are heard, and their efforts valued. By doing so, leaders build a sense of ownership and commitment among employees, enhancing their connection to the organization.

Effective leadership has a profound impact on employee retention. Leaders who can effectively communicate and embody the organization's core values create a positive and supportive work environment. This, in turn, leads to higher levels of job satisfaction, engagement, and loyalty among employees. When employees feel aligned with the organization's mission and values, they more likely stay with the company, reducing turnover rates and associated costs.

In times of change or crisis, strong leadership becomes particularly crucial. Effective leaders provide stability and direction, helping employees navigate uncertainties and remain focused on the organization's goals. Their ability to communicate a clear vision and maintain trust serves as an essential part of sustaining morale and retaining talent during challenging periods.

Effective leadership is indispensable for fostering a culture of retention within an organization. Leaders have responsibility to develop and maintain a positive culture, setting the stage for the organization's mission, vision, and core values, and ensuring that these values get communicated and lived each day. This alignment becomes particularly crucial for engaging and retaining Gen Y and Z employees, who prioritize purpose and integrity in their work. By demonstrating commitment to core values and creating an environment of trust and respect, leaders can enhance employee engagement, satisfaction, and loyalty. Ultimately, the strength of an organization's leadership provides a key determinant of its ability to attract and retain top talent, driving long-term success and stability.

Communication
Effective communication stands as a linchpin for retaining and engaging Gen Y and Z employees, who bring distinct expectations and preferences when it comes to communication, necessitating a strategic approach from organizational leaders to meet their needs and foster retention. These employees de-

mand open, honest, and continual feedback, viewing effective communication as essential to their professional growth, engagement, and overall satisfaction within the organization.

At the heart of effective communication lies transparency and authenticity. Gen Y and Z employees value leaders candid and forthcoming about organizational goals, challenges, and decisions. For example, leaders can foster transparency by regularly sharing company updates, financial performance metrics, and strategic initiatives through channels such as town hall meetings, company-wide emails, and intranet platforms. By providing visibility into the inner workings of the organization, leaders can build trust and credibility among younger employees, thereby enhancing retention.

Furthermore, Gen Y and Z employees crave continual feedback and recognition for their contributions. Unlike traditional annual performance reviews, which may feel disconnected and infrequent to these generations, ongoing feedback loops are preferred. Leaders can adopt strategies such as regular one-on-one check-ins, peer-to-peer feedback mechanisms, and real-time performance-tracking tools to provide timely and actionable feedback. Additionally, acknowledging and celebrating achievements, whether through public recognition, rewards, or personalized feedback, reinforces a culture of appreciation and engagement among younger employees.

In addition to transparency and feedback, technology plays a pivotal role in communication with Gen Y and Z employees. These digital natives have lived accustomed to seamless and instantaneous communication through various digital channels, including email, instant messaging, video conferencing, and social media. As such, organizations should leverage technology to facilitate communication and collaboration, providing platforms for virtual meetings, project management, and knowledge sharing. By embracing digital tools and platforms, leaders can cater to the preferences of younger employees and create a flexible and easily accessible communication environment. By creating an environment where all voices can be heard and valued, leaders can strengthen employee engagement and retention among younger generations.

Effective communication stands paramount to retaining Gen Y and Z employees in today's organizations. By prioritizing transparency, feedback, and technology in communication practices, leaders can create a culture where younger employees feel empowered, engaged, and motivated to contribute their talents and expertise. As organizations navigate the complexities of a multigenerational workforce, effective communication emerges as a cornerstone for driving retention and success among Generation Y and Generation Z employees.

Accountability

Accountability emerges as a fundamental element in increasing retention rates among Gen Y and Z employees, who place a high value on transparency, integrity, and a culture of accountability, viewing it as essential to fostering trust, collaboration, and overall satisfaction within the organization. When accountability becomes ingrained in the workplace culture, Gen Y and Z employees feel more empowered, engaged, and motivated to contribute their best work, thereby enhancing retention and driving organizational success.

Accountability holds particular importance to Gen Y and Z employees due to their desire for transparency and authenticity in the workplace. Unlike previous generations, who may have been accustomed to hierarchical structures and top-down decision-making, these younger cohorts seek environments where accountability gets distributed across all levels and individuals take ownership of their actions and outcomes. By fostering a culture of accountability, organizations demonstrate their commitment to honesty, integrity, and ethical conduct, thereby earning the trust and respect of Gen Y and Z employees.

High-performing teams that hold each other accountable earn high valuation from Gen Y and Z employees, as they recognize the collective impact of individual contributions and the importance of mutual support and collaboration. For example, in agile project management methodologies, teams operate as self-organizing and accountable for delivering on their commitments within set timeframes. This approach not only promotes accountability at the team level, but also cultivates a sense of shared responsibility and camaraderie among team members, leading to increased engagement and satisfaction.

Individuals within an organization can hold each other accountable in a positive manner by establishing clear expectations, providing constructive feedback, and recognizing and celebrating achievements. For instance, peer-to-peer accountability can be fostered through regular check-ins, collaborative goal-setting sessions, and peer coaching initiatives where team members support and challenge each other to excel. By creating a culture of mutual accountability, organizations empower employees to take ownership of their work and hold themselves and their peers to high standards of performance and conduct.

Gen Y and Z employees prefer a culture that holds each other accountable because it promotes fairness, transparency, and a shared commitment to excellence. In environments that embrace accountability, individuals feel valued and respected for their contributions, leading to higher levels of engagement, job satisfaction, and retention. Moreover, holding leaders in the organization accountable for their actions and words ranks as equally important to Gen Y and Z employees, as it reinforces the principles of integrity, trust, and ethical leadership within the organization.

Accountability plays a pivotal role in retaining Gen Y and Z employees by fostering a culture of transparency, collaboration, and shared responsibility. By promoting accountability at all levels of the organization and empowering individuals to hold themselves and their peers accountable, leaders can create an environment where employees feel motivated, engaged, and valued, ultimately driving retention and organizational success in today's dynamic workforce landscape.

> **Interesting Fact:** *PwC conducted a study of more than 40,000 workers from different generations and found that work-life balance was the top priority for Gen Y and Z workers. The study also found that these workers were more likely to leave their jobs if their employers did not provide the flexibility they desired. (LinkedIn, 2024)*

GABLES: INTRINSIC AND EXTRINSIC MOTIVATION

The gables of employee motivation sit atop the firm foundation of purpose, supported by authentic leadership, deliberate communication, and a clear system of accountability. High employee motivation results from a multitude of factors, but overall comprises intrinsic and extrinsic factors.

Intrinsic

Autonomy and trust remain key factors in creating a sense of value and intrinsic motivation. Creating and maintaining a healthy organizational environment becomes essential for retaining employees, particularly Gen Y and Z, who prioritize autonomy in their work and trust from leaders. Employees want to feel valued and respected without the unhealthy tension that comes from excessive micromanagement.

In such environments, outcomes of tasks hold a higher priority over how and when the work gets accomplished. Employees value the autonomy to manage their day-to-day activities. In many cases, due to the emergence of technology in today's environment, work can be accomplished from anywhere. A sense of autonomy breeds an environment of innovation and freedom to explore new ways of getting results.

Organizations that prioritize trust build strong, positive relationships with their employees. Trust, in essence, represents a two-way street between leaders and workers where someone can admit making a mistake, not knowing the answer, or are struggling, without fear of retribution. This degree of openness allows for a better understanding of competence and preparedness to take on new or complex assignments. It supports and encourages employees to take risks, innovate, and collaborate more effectively, leading to a more dynamic and productive work environment.

Employees who feel free from excessive micromanagement and stress become more likely to be engaged and productive. They also more often recommend their organization to others, contributing to a positive employer brand. Furthermore, a healthy organizational environment supports employee development and growth, providing opportunities for continuous learning and career advancement. This not only helps in retaining current employees but also attracts new talent to the organization.

Gen Y and Z remain particularly sensitive to the quality of their work environment. They value transparency, authenticity, and ethical behavior from their employers. These generations expect their organizations to uphold high moral standards and provide a supportive workplace. When they perceive a misalignment between their values and the organization's practices, they quickly seek opportunities elsewhere. On the other hand, when they experience a healthy organizational environment that aligns with their values, their commitment and loyalty to the organization increases significantly.

In the landscape of modern workplaces, a sense of relatedness and competence stands as a potent tool for retaining and engaging Gen Y and Z employees, who place a high value on recognition and acknowledgment of their contributions, viewing it as essential to their sense of worth within the organization. Leaders who understand and prioritize recognition can significantly improve retention rates among Gen Y and Z employees, fostering a culture of appreciation and empowerment that fuels long-term commitment and success.

Gen Y and Z employees demand recognition for their efforts and achievements, seeking validation and affirmation from their leaders and peers. This need for recognition stems from several factors, including a desire for validation, a craving for feedback and growth, and a need for a sense of belonging and purpose in the workplace. Recognizing the contributions of these employees not only boosts morale and engagement but also reinforces their commitment to the organization and its goals.

One effective recognition strategy for Gen Y and Z employees comes in providing regular and specific feedback on their work. Rather than waiting for annual performance reviews, leaders can offer timely praise and constructive feedback on a continuous basis, highlighting achievements, strengths, and areas for improvement. Additionally, personalized recognition, such as handwritten notes, public praise in team meetings, or personalized awards, can make employees feel valued and appreciated for their unique contributions.

Furthermore, organizations can leverage technology to facilitate recognition and appreciation among Gen Y and Z employees. Digital platforms and tools, such as social recognition platforms, employee recognition apps, and virtual recognition ceremonies, provide avenues for peer-to-peer recognition and celebration of achievements in real time. By harnessing the power of technology, leaders can create a culture of recognition that transcends physical boundaries and fosters a sense of camaraderie and belonging among remote and distributed teams.

Providing opportunities for career development and growth

represents another effective recognition strategy. Gen Y and Z employees value learning and development opportunities that enable them to enhance their skills and advance their careers. Leaders can recognize and invest in the potential of these employees by offering mentorship programs, skill-building workshops, and career progression pathways. By demonstrating a commitment to their professional development, organizations can show Gen Y and Z employees that their contributions are valued and that their future within the organization is promising.

Recognition plays a pivotal role in retaining Gen Y and Z employees by affirming their value, boosting their engagement, and reinforcing their commitment to the organization. It helps employees feel like a vital part of the organization's success. By understanding the unique preferences and motivations of these younger generations, leaders can implement tailored recognition strategies that resonate with their desires for feedback, growth, and appreciation. Through consistent and meaningful recognition efforts, organizations can create a culture where Gen Y and Z employees feel valued, engaged, and motivated to contribute their best work, ultimately driving retention and success in the long term.

Extrinsic

Extrinsic motivational factors comprise the organization's employee benefit and compensation program. In this chapter, we explore how the combination of comprehensive employee benefits and a nurturing, health-focused environment constitutes the structure of organizational culture, ultimately influencing employee engagement, productivity, and retention.

In the modern workforce, employee benefits have undergone significant transformation, especially in response to the evolving expectations of Gen Y and Z. These generations, now making up a substantial portion of the workforce, place high importance on comprehensive and competitive employee benefits. The shift in benefits expectations has been further accelerated by the COVID-19 pandemic, which redefined workplace norms and highlighted the need for flexible and holistic benefit packages. The access to technology has made it easier for employees to explore new job opportunities, placing additional pressure on organizations to offer competitive benefits to retain top talent. Here, we explore the importance of providing robust employee benefits to attract and retain Gen Y and Z, with examples of powerful modern-day employee benefits and emerging trends in the workplace.

Competitive employee benefits remain crucial for retaining Gen Y and Z employees, who have grown up with technology, enabling them to easily research and compare benefits offered by different employers. They value organizations that invest in their well-being, professional development, and work-life balance. The ability to quickly and effortlessly transition to companies that offer better benefits has made it imperative for organizations to stay ahead in the benefits game. Companies that fail to provide attractive and comprehensive benefits risk losing their most valuable assets to competitors.

Modern-day employee benefits have expanded beyond traditional offerings such as health insurance and retirement plans. For instance, remote work has become a significant trend, especially after the COVID-19 pandemic. Both Generation Y and Generation Z highly value the flexibility to work from home or any location of their choice. Remote work benefits not only include the flexibility of location but also flexible work hours, which help employees achieve a better work-life balance.

Retirement benefits represent another crucial aspect. With traditional pension plans becoming less common, employers increasingly offer 401(k) plans with matching contributions, financial planning services, and even student loan repayment assistance. These benefits help younger employees manage their finances and plan, making them more likely to stay with an organization long-term.

Employee health benefits have also evolved, with a greater emphasis on holistic wellness programs. Comprehensive health insurance, mental health support, wellness programs, gym memberships, and healthy snacks in the office are all part of modern health benefits that appeal to these generations. Mental health has become particularly important, and organizations that offer robust mental health support through counseling services and mental health days are viewed favorably.

Engagement and growth potential remain critical for retaining Gen Y and Z employees seeking meaningful work and opportunities for career advancement. Organizations that provide continuous training and development programs, mentorship opportunities, and clear career progression paths stand a better chance of retaining this young talent. For example, companies like Google and Microsoft offer extensive training programs and educational reimbursements, which rate as highly attractive to these generations.

Technology benefits are also crucial. Access to the latest technology, tech stipends, and opportunities to work on innovative projects can be significant draws. These employees expect their employers to be technologically advanced and to provide the tools necessary for efficient and effective work.

Compensation and bonuses remain fundamental but with a twist. Competitive base salaries remain essential, but these generations also look for performance-based bonuses, profit-sharing plans, and equity options. Financial recognition for their contributions may be crucial, but they also value the opportunity to share in the company's success.

Flexible work arrangements continue as a high priority. Beyond remote work, flexible hours, compressed workweeks, and job-sharing options cater to the desire for a better work-life balance. This flexibility helps employees manage their personal and professional lives more effectively, reducing burnout and increasing job satisfaction.

Professional development opportunities represent a key to retaining young talent. Organizations that invest in their employees' professional growth through workshops, conferences, certifications, and other learning opportunities demonstrate a commitment to their career advancement. This investment not only improves skills but also fosters loyalty.

Health and wellness initiatives have become more comprehensive. Beyond traditional health insurance, companies offer wellness programs that include mental health support, stress management workshops, fitness challenges, and on-site health screenings. These initiatives help employees maintain their physical and mental well-being, contributing to higher retention rates.

Work-life balance stands as a critical consideration for Gen Y and Z. They value employers who respect their personal time and offer benefits that support a healthy work-life balance. Policies such as generous parental leave, paid time off, and sabbaticals. These benefits contribute to employee satisfaction and retention.

Competitive employee benefits are essential for retaining Gen Y and Z in a highly competitive market. The ability to quickly transition to other organizations with better benefits makes it imperative for employers to offer comprehensive and attractive benefits packages. Modern employee benefits include remote work options, robust health and wellness programs, competitive retirement plans, opportunities for engagement and growth, access to the latest technology, attractive compensation and bonuses, flexible work arrangements, and professional development opportunities. Organizations that invest in these benefits demonstrate a commitment to their employees' well-being and career growth, fostering a positive organizational culture that retains top talent and drives long-term success.

THE TOXIC CULTURE— THE RETENTION "KILLER"

Interesting Fact: *Toxicity is rampant in the workplace. Almost two-thirds of working Americans say they have worked in a "toxic" workplace, with 26 percent of them saying they have worked in more than one.*[8] *Most blame that toxicity on poor management. (SHRM, 2024)*

In the realm of organizational culture, the presence of toxicity stands as a formidable threat to employee retention, particularly among Gen Y and 1Z employees. A toxic work environment, characterized by negativity, dysfunction, and a lack of support, can quickly erode morale and productivity and ultimately drive talented employees to seek employment elsewhere. Understanding the specific elements of toxic work cultures and their detrimental effects on retention presents a crucial requirement for organizations aiming to create a positive and engaging workplace environment that resonates with younger generations.

Poor leadership remains a hallmark of a toxic work culture, where managers exhibit authoritarian, micromanaging, or manipulative behaviors that undermine trust and erode employee morale. For example, a manager who belittles, intimidates, or plays favorites with certain employees creates an atmosphere of fear and resentment, leading to high turnover and low engagement levels. Additionally, organizational politics and favoritism can breed distrust and animosity among colleagues, fostering a toxic environment where employees feel undervalued and unappreciated.

Moreover, a lack of transparency and communication exacerbates toxic work cultures, as employees feel left in the dark about organizational decisions, changes, and expectations. When leaders withhold information, ignore feedback, or fail to address concerns effectively, it creates a breeding ground for rumors, gossip, and speculation, fueling feelings of uncertainty and disillusionment among employees. In such environments, Gen Y and Z employees, who value openness, honesty, and authenticity, are quick to disengage and seek alternate opportunities where their voices are heard and valued.

Furthermore, toxic work cultures often manifest in high levels of stress, burnout, and work-related pressure, as employees face unrealistic expectations, excessive workloads, and a lack of work-life balance. Whether a constant barrage of emails, tight deadlines, or a culture of presenteeism where long hours equal dedication, these stressors take a toll on employee well-being and satisfaction, driving them to prioritize their mental and physical health over their job. Gen Y and Z employees who prioritize work-life balance and holistic well-being become particularly sensitive to environments disregarding their need for self-care and personal fulfillment.

The pervasive negativity and toxicity of a work environment not only drive employees away but also tarnish the organization's reputation, making it difficult to attract top talent in the future. In today's age of social media and online reviews, disgruntled employees can easily share their negative experiences with the world, deterring prospective candidates from considering employment with the organization. As a result, organizations with toxic work cultures find themselves trapped in a vicious cycle of turnover, recruitment challenges, and reputational damage, hindering their ability to thrive in a competitive market.

Toxic work cultures pose a significant threat to employee retention, particularly among Gen Y and Z employees who seek positive, supportive, and inclusive workplace environments. By recognizing the specific elements of toxicity within an organization and taking proactive measures to address them, leaders can create a culture that fosters engagement, well-being, and retention among employees. From promoting ethical leadership and transparent communication to prioritizing employee well-being and work-life balance, organizations can mitigate the risks of toxicity and build a culture that attracts, retains, and empowers top talent in today's dynamic workforce landscape.

Now that you understand more about the Structure of Organizational Culture and how they are associated with retaining Gen Y and Z, it is time for your Self-Assessment. Look at the following assessment chart. How would you honestly rate yourself? As mentioned in your last assessment on leadership, if you find that you need some work in any given area, that's OK! The point is not to be "perfect" but to be willing to learn, change, and adapt to the complexity of what employees are demanding of managers and leaders. Again, embrace the journey—and continue to work on your own skillset, which will inevitably be appreciated by your employees.

ORGANIZATIONAL CULTURE STRATEGY ASSESSMENT

As a leader/manager in your organization, how would you rate yourself?			
Organizational Culture	**Doing Good**	**Needs Work**	**How can you improve?**
Develops and communicates well-defined organizational core values			
Implements modern and attractive employee benefits— Reviews and updates continually to remain competitive			
Creates an autonomous environment			

(continued)

Organizational Culture	Doing Good	Needs Work	How can you improve?
Provides open, honest, and continual feedback using all forms of communication methods			
Provides continual recognition and acknowledgment of employee contributions			
Communicates and creates a shared vision that inspires and unites employees			
Holds self and others accountable, remains open to others holding you accountable			

Chapter 6 explores the pivotal role organizational culture plays in employee retention, particularly among Generation Y (Millennials) and Generation Z (Zoomers). Culture is described as the "heartbeat" of an organization, shaping its identity, values, and behaviors while profoundly influencing employee satisfaction, engagement, and loyalty. A strong, positive culture is not just beneficial but essential for attracting and retaining top talent, whereas a toxic culture can lead to high turnover and reputational damage.

SUMMARY OF CHAPTER 6: THE FORCE OF CULTURE

The chapter presents the Structure of Organizational Culture through three key components: Foundation, Pillars, and Gables.

- **The Foundation** comprises the organization's mission and values, providing a sense of purpose and direction. Gen Y and Z employees seek alignment between their personal values and the organization's mission, driving loyalty and engagement. Clear values such as integrity, innovation, and teamwork help shape behavior and decision-making, while fostering a sense of belonging.

- **The Pillars**—Leadership, Communication, and Accountability—are essential for supporting a positive culture. Leadership plays a central role in modeling and upholding core values, while effective communication ensures transparency and fosters trust. Accountability, valued by younger generations, promotes fairness, integrity, and a collaborative environment where individuals feel respected and empowered.

- **The Gables** represent the dual motivators of intrinsic and extrinsic rewards. Intrinsic motivators like autonomy, trust, and recognition contribute to a sense of purpose and engagement, while extrinsic factors such as competitive benefits, work-life balance, and compensation address tangible employee needs. A balanced approach helps organizations retain top talent.

Practical strategies for building and maintaining a positive culture include developing and communicating clear core values, offering modern and competitive benefits, fostering open communication, providing continual recognition, and holding leaders accountable. The chapter concludes with a self-assessment tool to help leaders evaluate and improve their cultural strategies, emphasizing the importance of adaptability and ongoing learning.

KEY BULLET POINTS

- **Organizational Culture's Role:** Shapes employee engagement, satisfaction, and retention.

- **Structure of Culture:**
  - *Foundation*: Mission and values create purpose and alignment.
  - *Pillars*: Leadership, communication, and accountability sustain the culture.
  - *Gables*: Intrinsic (autonomy, trust) and extrinsic (benefits, compensation) motivators drive engagement.

- **Positive Culture Benefits:** Fosters loyalty, collaboration, and performance.

- **Toxic Culture Effects:**
  - Poor leadership and lack of transparency drive disengagement.
  - High stress and work-life imbalance increase turnover.

- **Strategies for Improvement:**
  - › Communicate clear values.
  - › Offer competitive benefits and flexible arrangements.
  - › Foster open, honest communication.
  - › Recognize and reward employee contributions.
  - › Ensure accountability at all levels.

KEY SKILLS AND APPROACHES

- **Leadership:** Model core values and provide consistent direction.
- **Communication:** Maintain transparency and engage in continuous feedback.
- **Recognition:** Regularly acknowledge and celebrate achievements.
- **Flexibility:** Adapt benefits and work arrangements to meet modern employee expectations.
- **Self-Reflection:** Use tools to assess and improve cultural strategies.
- **Accountability:** Promote fairness and collaboration through shared responsibility.
- **Autonomy and Trust:** Empower employees to take ownership of their work.

QUESTIONS FOR DEEPER UNDERSTANDING

1. How does your organization's mission align with the personal values of your employees?
2. What are the key signs that your workplace culture might be turning toxic?
3. How can leaders effectively balance intrinsic and extrinsic motivators to enhance employee satisfaction?
4. What steps can be taken to ensure accountability at all levels of the organization?

5. How do clear and well-communicated core values contribute to employee retention?
6. What role do modern benefits and work-life balance play in attracting and retaining Gen Y and Z employees?
7. How can technology be leveraged to improve communication and recognition in a hybrid work environment?
8. What strategies can leaders use to address and transform a toxic workplace culture?
9. How does continual feedback impact employee engagement and motivation?
10. How can leaders assess whether their organization's culture is aligned with current workforce expectations?

CHAPTER 7

THE FORCE OF PEOPLE DEVELOPMENT

THE EXECUTIVE VIEWPOINT

Alexandra Wisenall, DNP, MBA, APRN, FNP-BC
WVU Medicine, East
Assistant Vice President, Ambulatory Operations of
System Medical Group
TOPIC: How Employee Training and Development
Improves Gen Y and Z Retention

Training and development can improve employee retention across all generations; the key is to understand the most important core values of each generation. Having this concept will help guide you to tailor each individual employee's training and development journey within your organization and/or workplace. Training and development examples can include (but are not limited to) the onboarding process, technical skills training, management training, and leadership development. I will never forget my first nursing manager and the comments she made to me during my interview. I was a new, 20-year-old (Gen Y) registered nurse applying for an RN position in a Level I Trauma Center Emergency Department. I was passionate, I was hungry, and, most of all, I was curious.

She said, "You can train anyone to do any skill, but you can't train attitude." That was the first encounter where I learned the impact of your attitude and how it can affect not only your own perception but also others. Thus began my nursing career as a brand-new emergency room RN. But this statement was influential and has stuck with me throughout the progression of my career. Most recently, I heard a similar quote from the hit TV show

"Ted Lasso," where the main character was coaching his team and shared, "Be curious, not judgmental." Curiosity is the secret sauce; generational core values are the main ingredients. Being equipped with this recipe combination is essential for an organization's successful retention course.

Let's explore Generation Y (Millennials); this generation is tech-savvy, responsive to feedback, and values flexibility, attention, "work-life" balance, and meaningful motivation. Understanding these core values can help you develop a training and development plan that incorporates each of these factors so that your Generation Y employee feels connected and engaged, thus increasing their likelihood of retention with the company. In layman's terms, we (the Millennials) like to be innovators—give us the space, freedom, and trust to do our best work, but please give consistent feedback and positive praise so we have the reassurance that we are doing our best work. Generation Z has many similar values to us Millennials, but they have also been known to have a focus on social responsibility, generational diversity, and ethics. Creating opportunities where these employees can be integrated to influence the workplace culture can also help to fulfill these core value areas.

Ultimately, what Generation Y & Z want was outlined in psychologist Abraham Maslow's pyramid of the five levels of human needs, and these generations have been brave enough to ask for them. Now as employers, we must have the courage to listen and tailor our techniques to not just meet these needs but to retain organizational talent.

Employee development serves as the catalyst for organizational growth and employee retention. In this chapter, we delve into how offering robust employee development opportunities directly impacts and increases retention rates, exploring the connection between career growth, skills enhancement, and a strong commitment to staying with the company.

The topic of employee development sometimes gets confused by the outdated concept of the career ladder. Over the years, organizations have become very flat. In the past, the corporate environment modeled the military rank system (Figure 5.). An individual would enter the workplace in an entry-level position and, throughout the years, would progress through a variety of positions until reaching their pinnacle as a vice president or a president of an organization. This process would take decades to accomplish.

The modern workplace has significantly changed (Figure 6). Organizations have reduced the number of levels between an entry level position to the president of the organization. What used to be 10 or 15 rungs on the corporate career ladder are now between 5 and 8 rungs to maximize an individual's progression.

TRADITIONAL ORGANIZATION CHART

Figure 5. Traditional Organization Chart

MODERN ORGANIZATION CHART

Figure 6. Modern Organization Chart

Accepted wisdom holds that Gen Y and Z employees look for urgency in their career advancement. In truth, a sense of reality supersedes any sense of urgency. Gen Y and Z employees entering the workforce in entry level positions look at organizational charts that have very few opportunities for advancement. Therefore, retaining employees with minimal advancement opportunities has become a significant challenge for any organization. As a result, organizations need to be very sensitive to what career advancement opportunities exist within the organization and appropriately communicate them so employees understand what the future may hold.

The balance between career advancement opportunities and employee retention lies with employee development. There is no doubt that Gen Y and Z employees are ambitious and seek opportunities for career growth and advancement. Employee development programs provide avenues for acquiring new skills, knowledge, and experiences essential for progressing in their careers. These generations value organizations that invest in their professional development and offer pathways for upward mobility. Providing opportunities for employee development enhances job satisfaction and engagement among Gen Y and Z employees. When organizations invest in their growth and provide avenues for learning and development, employees feel valued, motivated, and committed to their roles. This sense of fulfillment contributes to higher levels of job satisfaction and retention within the organization.

With the rapid pace of technological advancements and industry changes, Gen Y and Z employees recognize the importance of continuously upgrading their technical skills and staying relevant in the job market. Employee development initiatives equip them with the tools, training, and resources needed to adapt to evolving job roles, emerging technologies, and shifting market trends.

Gen Y and Z employees also prioritize personal and professional fulfillment in their careers. Employee development programs enable them to pursue their passions, interests, and goals, whether that means acquiring new skills, exploring different roles, or pursuing advanced education. By investing in their development, organizations support the holistic well-being and fulfillment of their employees.

THE PATH TO EMPLOYEE DEVELOPMENT

Gen Y and Z employee development programs and strategies remain essential for nurturing talent, fostering growth, and retaining valuable employees in today's dynamic workforce. Some effective programs and strategies tailored to the needs and preferences of Gen Y and Z employees include:

- **Mentorship Programs:** Implement mentorship programs that pair younger employees with experienced mentors within the organization. This facilitates knowledge transfer, skill development, and career guidance while also providing opportunities for networking and relationship-building.

- **Cross-Training Initiatives:** Offer cross-training opportunities that allow employees to gain exposure to different roles, departments, and functions within the organization. This helps broaden their skill sets, deepen their understanding of the business, and prepare them for future leadership positions.

- **Continuous Learning and Development:** Provide access to continuous learning and development resources, such as workshops, seminars, webinars, and online courses. Gen Y and Z employees value opportunities for ongoing skill enhancement and professional growth, making a variety of learning options key.

- **Leadership Development Programs:** Offer leadership development programs specifically designed for younger employees who show potential for leadership roles. These programs can include training on leadership skills, decision-making, conflict resolution, and emotional intelligence.

- **Feedback and Coaching:** Implement regular feedback and coaching sessions to support the development of Gen Y and Z employees. Provide constructive feedback, guidance, and support to help them reach their full potential and navigate their career paths effectively.

- **Flexible Career Paths:** Offer flexible career paths that allow employees to explore different roles, projects, and career trajectories within the organization. Gen Y and Z employees value flexibility and autonomy in their careers, so providing opportunities for exploration and growth is essential.

- **Technology-Based Learning Platforms:** Leverage technology-based learning platforms and tools to deliver training and development programs in a convenient and accessible manner. Gen Y and Z employees are digital natives who appreciate the flexibility and convenience of online learning.

- **Recognition and Rewards:** Implement recognition and rewards programs to celebrate the achievements and contributions of Gen Y and Gen Z employees. Recognizing their efforts and accomplishments motivates them to continue striving for excellence and reinforces a culture of appreciation and engagement.

By implementing these employee development programs and strategies, organizations can effectively support the growth, development, and retention of Generation Y and Generation Z talent, ultimately driving organizational success in the long run.

TAILORING DEVELOPMENT PROGRAMS TO EMPLOYEE NEEDS

Although it is beneficial to offer a variety of employee development programs, organizations must also customize those programs to the individual employee's needs. In doing so, the organization can maximize efforts to specifically develop individuals, to the benefit of both the organization and the employee.

INDIVIDUALIZED DEVELOPMENT PLANS

Crafting individualized development plans for Generation Y and Generation Z employees offers numerous benefits that contribute to their professional growth, engagement, and retention within the organization. These younger generations value personalized experiences and opportunities tailored to their unique skills, interests, and career aspirations. By creating individualized development plans, organizations can address the specific needs and preferences of each employee, fostering a sense of ownership, investment, and commitment to their growth and development.

A key benefit of individualized development plans comes in enabling employees to take ownership of their careers and chart their own paths for growth. By involving employees in the development process and considering their input, interests, and goals, organizations empower them to identify areas for improvement, set meaningful objectives, and pursue opportunities aligned with their aspirations. This sense of ownership motivates Gen Y and Z employees to take initiative, engage proactively in their development, and invest in their long-term success within the organization.

Furthermore, individualized development plans foster a culture of continuous learning and growth, traits highly valued by Gen Y and Z employees. These younger generations seek opportunities for skill enhancement, knowledge acquisition, and career advancement. By customizing development plans to address employees' specific learning needs and career goals, organizations demonstrate their commitment to supporting their professional development journey. This personalized approach not only enhances employee engagement and satisfaction but also increases retention rates by providing meaningful opportunities for growth and advancement.

Moreover, individualized development plans promote talent retention by recognizing and leveraging employees' unique strengths, talents, and interests. By identifying and capitalizing on each employee's strengths, organizations can maximize their potential contributions and drive performance excellence. Additionally, aligning development plans with employees' interests and career aspirations increases job satisfaction and loyalty, as employees feel valued, understood, and invested in by their organization. This personalized approach to development builds a strong foundation for long-term employee engagement, loyalty, and retention, ultimately benefiting both the individual and the organization.

Designing and implementing tailored development programs for Gen Y and Z employees requires a strategic approach that addresses their unique needs, preferences, and aspirations. Here are the key steps for creating effective development programs:

- **Understand Their Needs:** Begin by conducting thorough research and analysis to understand the specific needs, preferences, and motivations of Gen Y and Z employees. Consider factors such as their learning styles, career goals, and areas for development. Engage with employees through surveys, focus groups, and one-on-one discussions to gather insights and feedback.

- **Set Clear Objectives:** Define clear objectives and goals for the development program based on the identified needs and priorities of Gen Y and Z employees. These objectives should align with the organization's overall strategic goals and objectives. Establish measurable outcomes and success criteria to track the effectiveness of the program.

- **Customize Development Plans:** Develop individualized development plans for each employee tailored to their skills, interests, and career aspirations. Work collaboratively with employees to identify their strengths, areas for improvement, and growth opportunities. Consider offering a mix of formal training, mentorship, on-the-job learning, and stretch assignments to provide a well-rounded development experience.

- **Provide Learning Opportunities:** Offer a variety of learning opportunities and resources to accommodate different learning styles and preferences. This may include workshops, seminars, online courses, coaching sessions, and job shadowing experiences. Leverage technology-based learning platforms to provide convenient and accessible learning options for Gen Y and Z employees.

- **Promote Continuous Feedback:** Establish a culture of continuous feedback and coaching to support the development of Gen Y and Z employees. Provide regular feedback on their performance, progress, and areas for improvement. Encourage open communication and dialogue between employees and their managers to address any challenges or concerns.

- **Encourage Collaboration and Networking:** Foster opportunities for collaboration, networking, and knowledge sharing among Gen Y and Z employees. Encourage cross-functional teamwork, peer mentoring, and community involvement to expand their professional networks and learn from diverse perspectives.

- **Measure and Evaluate Impact:** Monitor and evaluate the effectiveness of the development program on an ongoing basis. Collect data and feedback from participants to assess the program's impact on employee engagement, performance, and retention. Use this information to adjust and improve the program as needed.

- **Celebrate Success:** Recognize and celebrate the achievements and milestones of Gen Y and Z employees throughout their development journey. Acknowledge their progress, growth, and contributions to the organization. Celebrating success reinforces a culture of appreciation, engagement, and continuous improvement.

By following these steps, organizations can design and implement tailored development programs that effectively meet the needs of Generation Y and Generation Z employees, driving their professional growth, engagement, and retention within the organization.

INDIVIDUALIZED COACHING

The rise of individual coaching for Gen Y and Z employees represents a significant shift in how organizations approach talent development and retention. In an era that highly values personalized experiences, individual coaching sessions offer a tailored and focused approach to supporting the growth and development of employees. Experienced and certified trained coaches who specialize in working with younger generations, understanding their unique needs, motivations, and aspirations lead these sessions. By providing one-on-one coaching, organizations demonstrate their commitment to investing in the professional development and success of their Gen Y and Gen Z employees.

Individual coaching sessions offer a personalized development experience that addresses the specific goals, challenges, and opportunities of each employee. Unlike traditional training programs or group workshops, individual coaching allows employees to receive customized guidance, support, and feedback tailored to their individual needs and preferences. Coaches work closely with employees to identify their strengths, areas for improvement, and career aspirations, providing personalized strategies and action plans to help them reach their full potential.

Individual coaching sessions provide a safe and confidential space for employees to explore their personal and professional development goals. This level of privacy and confidentiality encourages open and honest conversations, allowing employees to address sensitive topics, overcome obstacles, and explore new possibilities without fear of judgment or reprisal. Coaches serve as trusted advisors and mentors, offering guidance, perspective, and encouragement to help employees navigate their career paths effectively.

Furthermore, individual coaching sessions contribute to talent retention by fostering a strong sense of commitment, loyalty, and engagement among Gen Y and Z employees. When employees receive personalized support and guidance from a coach who understands their unique needs and aspirations, they feel valued, supported, and invested in by their organization. This sense of appreciation and recognition strengthens the employee-employer relationship, leading to higher levels of job satisfaction, loyalty, and retention.

In conclusion, individual coaching for Gen Y and Z employees offers a powerful tool for supporting their professional development and retention within the organization. By offering personalized guidance, support, and feedback, organizations demonstrate their commitment to investing in the success of their employees, ultimately driving engagement, satisfaction, and long-term loyalty. As the demand for personalized development experiences continues to rise, individual coaching represents a valuable strategy for organizations looking to attract, retain, and develop top talent in today's competitive job market.

FEEDBACK AND GOAL ALIGNMENT

Continuous feedback and aligning development goals with organizational objectives stand as critical components of developing and retaining Generation Y and Generation Z employees in today's workforce. These younger generations value transparency, clarity, and purpose in their work, and effective feedback mechanisms and goal alignment serve as key drivers of their engagement, motivation, and commitment to the organization.

Continuous feedback provides Gen Y and Z employees with timely insights into their performance, progress, and areas for improvement. Unlike traditional annual performance reviews, which may feel outdated and disconnected from day-to-day realities, continuous feedback fosters ongoing communication and dialogue between employees and their managers. This frequent exchange of feedback allows employees to receive real-time guidance, support, and recognition, enabling them to course-correct, improve, and grow in their roles. By providing continuous feedback, organizations demonstrate their commitment to supporting the development and success of their employees, ultimately driving engagement, satisfaction, and retention.

Furthermore, aligning development goals with organizational objectives ensures that employees' growth and development efforts tie directly to the strategic priorities and mission of the organization. When employees understand how their individual goals and contributions contribute to the larger goals of the organization, they feel a sense of purpose, significance, and alignment with the company's mission and values. This clarity of purpose motivates Gen Y and Z employees to invest their time, energy, and talents in meaningful ways that drive business outcomes and advance organizational success.

Moreover, aligning development goals with organizational objectives helps organizations maximize the impact and effectiveness of their talent development efforts. By focusing on the skills, competencies, and behaviors most critical to achieving organizational goals, organizations can prioritize their development initiatives and resources accordingly. This strategic alignment ensures that employees gain the knowledge, skills, and capabilities needed to drive business results and address emerging challenges and opportunities.

Continuous feedback and aligning development goals with organizational objectives represent essential strategies for developing and retaining Gen Y and Z employees. By providing ongoing feedback and clarity of purpose, organizations can foster a culture of growth, engagement, and alignment that empowers employees to thrive and succeed in their roles. As organizations continue to adapt to the evolving needs and preferences of younger generations, continuous feedback and goal alignment remain key priorities for driving employee development and retention in the modern workplace.

THE RIPPLE EFFECT OF DEVELOPMENT ON RETENTION

EMPLOYEE ENGAGEMENT AND JOB SATISFACTION

Employee engagement, job satisfaction, and retention closely interlink to significantly impact the success and longevity of Gen Y and Z employees within an organization. Younger generations place a high value on workplace satisfaction, meaningful work, and opportunities for growth and development. As these needs are met, employees become more engaged, satisfied, and committed to their roles and the organization.

Employee engagement refers to the level of emotional commitment and investment that employees have toward their work and the organization. Engaged employees are passionate, motivated, and dedicated to achieving their goals and contributing to the success of the organization. For Gen Y and Z employees, engagement closely ties to factors such as job autonomy, meaningful work, opportunities for learning and development, and a positive work environment. Engaged employees perform at their best, collaborate effectively with colleagues, and demonstrate a strong sense of loyalty and dedication to the organization.

Job satisfaction, another critical factor in retaining Gen Y and Z employees, refers to the overall contentment and fulfillment that employees experience in their roles. Work-life balance, recognition and rewards, career advancement opportunities, and alignment with organizational values and culture influence job satisfaction for younger generations. When employees feel satisfied with their jobs, they remain more committed to the organization, experience higher levels of morale and motivation, and exhibit greater loyalty and retention.

Retention, the final piece of the puzzle, refers to the ability of an organization to keep its employees over time, as influenced by factors such as engagement, job satisfaction, career development opportunities, and organizational culture. For

Gen Y and Z employees, retention means more than staying in a job; it means about staying with an organization that values their contributions, supports their growth and development, and provides a positive and fulfilling work experience. When organizations prioritize employee engagement, job satisfaction, and retention strategies tailored to the needs of younger generations, they create a work environment where employees feel valued, supported, and motivated to stay and grow.

The correlation between employee engagement, job satisfaction, and retention is crucial for the success and longevity of Gen Y and Z employees within an organization. By prioritizing factors that contribute to engagement and satisfaction, such as meaningful work, opportunities for development, and a positive work environment, organizations can foster a culture of engagement, satisfaction, and retention that enables them to attract, retain, and develop top talent in today's competitive job market.

TALENT RETENTION IN A COMPETITIVE MARKET

Offering development opportunities positions organizations as attractive employers in competitive talent markets, especially when targeting Gen Y and Z employees who prioritize growth and advancement in their careers. These younger generations feel drawn to organizations that invest in their professional development and offer pathways for learning, skill enhancement, and career progression. By prioritizing development opportunities, organizations not only attract top talent but also retain them by fostering a culture of continuous learning, growth, and advancement.

For Gen Y and Z employees, the availability of development opportunities represent a key factor in their decision-making process when considering potential employers. These younger generations seek organizations that offer formal training programs, mentorship opportunities, tuition reimbursement, and other resources for skill enhancement and career advancement. When organizations demonstrate a commitment to investing in their employees' growth and development, potential candidates feel valued, supported, and positioned for success within the organization.

Moreover, offering development opportunities helps organizations differentiate themselves as employers of choice in competitive talent markets. In today's job market, marked by talent shortages and skill gaps, organizations that prioritize employee development gain a competitive edge in attracting top talent. By offering robust development programs and resources, organizations demonstrate their commitment to nurturing talent, building capability, and driving innovation. This positions them as employers who not only offer attractive compensation and benefits but also invest in their employees' long-term success and career growth.

Furthermore, providing development opportunities plays a crucial role in retaining Gen Y and Z employees once onboarded. These younger generations more likely stay with organizations that offer opportunities for learning, growth, and advancement. By investing in their employees' development, organizations create a sense of loyalty, engagement, and commitment that fosters long-term retention. Employees who feel supported in their professional growth more likely remain with the organization, contribute to its success, and become advocates for its culture and values.

In summary, offering development opportunities stands as an essential element in positioning organizations as attractive employers in competitive talent markets, particularly when targeting Gen Y and Z employees. By prioritizing employee development, organizations not only attract top talent but also retain it by creating a culture of continuous learning, growth, and advancement. This investment in employee development not only benefits individuals but also drives organizational success and competitiveness in the long run.

Employee development extends beyond an investment in skills—it demonstrates an investment in loyalty and longevity. Offering development opportunities shows a commitment to employees' growth and future within the organization. In return, employees feel compelled to reciprocate that commitment by choosing to stay and contribute their best to the company's success.

The key takeaway? Employee development represents a retention superpower. It empowers employees to envision a future with their current employer, equips them with the skills needed for success, and fosters a sense of belonging and purpose. In today's competitive landscape, organizations that prioritize employee development can not only retain their talent but also thrive and innovate in an ever-evolving world of work.

As you have done with the last two chapters, it is time to assess what you are doing with the people in your organization to help retain them.

PEOPLE DEVELOPMENT STRATEGY ASSESSMENT

As a leader/manager in your organization, how would you rate yourself?			
People Strategy	**Doing Good**	**Needs Work**	**How can you improve?**
Develop a clear and defined organizational chart available to employees			
Provide employee development opportunities that include training, certifications, external job enrichment initiatives, personalized coaching, etc.			
Have personalized development plans for employees			

(continued)

People Strategy	Doing Good	Needs Work	How can you improve?
Develop agreed-upon and defined job expectations			
Promote continuous feedback toward job expectations			

SUMMARY OF CHAPTER 7: THE FORCE OF PEOPLE DEVELOPMENT

Chapter 7 explores the critical role of employee training and development in retaining Generation Y (Millennials) and Generation Z (Zoomers) employees. It emphasizes that robust development opportunities not only enhance job satisfaction and engagement but also foster loyalty and a sense of purpose, vital elements in today's competitive talent market. The chapter underscores the importance of tailoring training programs to align with the core values of these younger generations.

Generations Y and Z value autonomy, flexibility, feedback, and opportunities for personal and professional growth. They seek organizations that invest in their development, provide pathways for advancement, and foster a positive workplace culture. Training and development strategies should focus on technical skills, leadership development, mentorship, and cross-functional training. Programs that cater to social responsibility, diversity, and ethical practices further resonate with these cohorts.

The chapter challenges the outdated concept of the corporate "ladder," highlighting the shift to flatter organizational structures. With fewer hierarchical levels, employers must create innovative career pathways and communicate opportunities clearly. Individualized development plans and continuous feedback stand out as essential tools for nurturing talent and fostering commitment.

Employee development programs such as mentorship, cross-training, and leadership workshops enable employees to enhance their skills, broaden their experiences, and align their growth with organizational objectives. Tailored approaches, such as one-on-one coaching and personalized learning paths, meet the diverse needs of employees and help build trust and engagement. Continuous feedback, goal alignment, and recognition are key to ensuring employees feel valued and motivated.

Finally, the chapter highlights that investing in employee development represent a strategic advantage in retaining top talent. Development initiatives not only equip employees with the skills to succeed but also demonstrate the organization's commitment to their growth. This fosters loyalty, reduces turnover, and positions the organization as an employer of choice.

KEY BULLET POINTS

- **Generational Values:**
  - › *Millennials (Gen Y)*: Value feedback, flexibility, innovation, and work-life balance.
  - › *Gen Z*: Prioritize social responsibility, diversity, and ethical practices.

- **Importance of Development:**
  - › Development programs foster job satisfaction, engagement, and retention.
  - › Tailored approaches resonate with individual needs and aspirations.
  - › **Training and Development Strategies:**
  - › Mentorship programs for knowledge transfer and networking.

- › Cross-training for broader skillsets and leadership preparation.
- › Leadership development focused on emotional intelligence and decision-making.

- ■ **Modern Career Pathways:**
  - › Flatter organizational structures require creative career advancement opportunities.
  - › Continuous learning keeps employees relevant and engaged.

- ■ **Retention through Development:**
  - › Personalized coaching and development plans align with career goals.
  - › Feedback and recognition reinforce commitment and motivation.

KEY SKILLS AND APPROACHES

- ■ **Individualized Development:** Craft personalized plans based on strengths, interests, and career aspirations.
- ■ **Mentorship:** Facilitate knowledge sharing and guidance from experienced employees.
- ■ **Cross-Training:** Offer exposure to various roles for skill diversification.
- ■ **Continuous Feedback:** Establish regular performance check-ins and constructive discussions.
- ■ **Leadership Development:** Train future leaders in skills such as decision-making, conflict resolution, and strategic thinking.
- ■ **Flexibility in Learning:** Utilize technology for accessible, self-paced training opportunities.
- ■ **Recognition:** Regularly acknowledge contributions to build morale and loyalty.

QUESTIONS FOR DEEPER UNDERSTANDING

1. How can organizations design training programs that align with the unique values of Gen Y and Z employees?
2. What strategies can employers use to communicate advancement opportunities in flat organizational structures?
3. How do personalized development plans impact employee engagement and retention?
4. What role does continuous feedback play in fostering employee satisfaction and growth?
5. How can organizations balance technical training with leadership and soft skills development?
6. In what ways can mentorship programs benefit both mentors and mentees within an organization?
7. How does recognition and reward influence the retention of younger employees?
8. What innovative approaches can organizations adopt to create meaningful career pathways for Gen Y and Z?
9. How do employee development programs contribute to a company's competitive edge in talent acquisition?
10. What systems or tools can organizations implement to provide effective, technology-based learning opportunities?

CHAPTER 8

INCREASE
THE ODDS

THE EXECUTIVE VIEWPOINT

Navin Parmar, BE (Hons), MBA
Co-Founder and Vice President, Interlink Analytics, Inc.
Senior Data and AI Executive, Microsoft Inc.

For both Generations Y and Z, workplace culture and values are held in high importance, but for different reasons. It seems from this data that what Generation Y (Millennials) employees want is a workplace culture that reflects personal values, focusing on teamwork, collaboration, and community. They will probably be extremely loyal to organizations that have an assuredly inclusive culture to which they feel belonging and with which they feel purpose.

On the other hand, flexibility, diversity, and innovation are more likely to be favored by Gen Z employees in the workplace culture. Several studies found that they want to work for companies that show corporate social responsibility and environmental concern. (Rank & Contreras, 2021). It is also expected that this generation will demand more transparency and authenticity from their employers, believe in open communication, and expect leaders who lead by consensus rather than authority.

The company needs to find a balance in retaining both generations, aiming for a culture of collaboration, purpose, innovation, and flexibility. For example, in the consulting environment, as I have faced usually on Fridays, Gen Y employees love team-building exercises and to take internal development classes to dedicate their time to socializing with their colleagues and discussing group accomplishments and problems. On the other hand, Gen Z employees tend to appreciate those corporate cultures that spur innovation and creativity, thus helping to promote a community spirit. They would prefer spending Fridays on something they like. The leadership style that will be more attractive to them is the one that appears driven by consensus with a strong mentorship and guidance scaffolding, as Stanford describes as "service leadership."(Stanford).

JOB SECURITY VS. JOB SATISFACTION

Gen Y employees give a higher weight to factors such as job security compared with immediate job satisfaction, which may be seen as insignificant. Job security is a major career decision criterion for the majority of, for example, Gen Y employees. They tend to prefer long-term stability if they feel secure in their job position and have a certain level of career growth through job mobility. Lifelong employment is, therefore, likely to continue, particularly with companies that provide stable work environments with the necessary career pathways and internal growth opportunities. (Chamchan & Kittisuksathit, 2019). An example of this can be seen in long-term employees who prioritize stable work environments, even in high-demand sectors like consulting, where job hopping is common.

In contrast, Gen Z prioritizes job satisfaction ahead of job security, making them more willing to jump ship and explore better opportunities if they feel their present role does not challenge them or advance their career ambitions (Masood, 2024). For instance, a Gen Z in a tech startup could leave a short time after joining an organization if it does not provide opportunities to grow or the scope and environment for continuous innovation—the need that I mentioned earlier. By my observations and research, this generation of employees is less concerned about job security and more focused on finding jobs that provide immediate job satisfaction, challenges, and an opportunity to make a difference.

And if we wanted to keep Gen Zs, of course, we've ensured we have roles that challenge and fulfill, with clear paths for promotion and development and the flexibility to find a new one if it doesn't work out. Taking on small incremental projects that would be satisfying to complete, trailing them down the road, and retaining them with a smile was a way to sustain the effort that led to success in difficult consulting careers.

WORK-LIFE BALANCE

Work-life balance management matters for both generations, but its forms differ for each. Gen Y employees usually pursue a balance that enables them to enjoy their employment while fulfilling their private affairs. In a consulting career, Millennials might use Fridays to focus on internal development and team bonding, ensuring they feel connected to the company while also addressing their personal growth (Bhuiyan et al., 2023). For example, a Gen Y employee might prefer to engage in professional development sessions or casual team activities on Fridays, which allows them to recharge and feel part of a cohesive team.

On the other hand, Gen Z rather focuses on their personal time and their flexibility. They want to finish the work within a particular time frame but if they have to work beyond the usual hours, they can do so on Mondays to Thursdays and take Fridays in the afternoon off to do things such as ride a bicycle or go out for a hike. This kind of flexibility is viewed as non-negotiable, and withholding it is perceived as an affront to their overall job happiness (Syahputra & Hendarman, 2024). For example, a Gen Z staff may be more interested in a job that has flexible hours rather than fixed hours with higher pay.

CAREER ADVANCEMENT AND DEVELOPMENT

Career advancement and development remain crucial for retaining Gen Y and Z employees, though their expectations differ. Gen Y employees typically look for structured career paths with clear milestones and the potential for long-term growth within the organization. (Hassan et al., 2020). My experience has led me to provide them with opportunities for professional development, mentorship, and leadership roles, and they are more likely to stay with a company that offers these opportunities. In my career, guiding the Millennials meant helping them establish their professional mastery by providing opportunities for training and certification. Helping them in providing mentorship to move to the next level in their career. We would also assist in management vs. technical leadership positions and develop long term guidance based on interest.

Gen Z employees, while also interested in career advancement, prefer roles that offer immediate challenges and the opportunity to learn new skills. Less concerned with long-term stability and more focused on gaining diverse experiences that will help them build a versatile skill set, this generation values mentorship but expects it to be more of a partnership where they have the freedom to explore new ideas and approaches. I remember working with one Gen Z where he wanted to have independence on how he performed the work and deliver on the outcome. He was less interested in my thoughts on how but more in what the end deliverable would be.

To retain both generations, organizations should provide tailored career development programs that meet the needs of each generation. For Gen Y, this might involve offering leadership training and long-term career planning, while for Gen Z, it could include rotational programs, opportunities for cross-functional projects, and access to continuous learning resources.

Retaining employees from both Gen Y and Z calls for a more complex approach, taking into consideration that they differ in values, expectations, and career pursuits. An organization should achieve a workplace atmosphere that effectively balances stability with flexibility, career development opportunities, and respect for work-life balance in order to create an atmosphere in which both generations feel valued, challenged, and motivated to stay.

Interesting fact: *According to SHRM 2024 Talent Trend Report, 54% of organizations use pre-employment assessments to gauge applicants' knowledge, skills, and abilities during the hiring process. While 78% say these assessments have improved the quality of their organization's hires, 36% also say these assessments have increased their time-to-fill.*

As we conclude this book on employee retention, we must emphasize that while our focus has primarily been on strategies for retaining current employees, the foundation of successful retention begins with hiring the right employees in the first place. The significance of hiring individuals who represent the right fit for the organization cannot be overstated, as it plays a critical role in enhancing overall retention rates. When organizations invest in recruiting individuals whose values, skills, and attitudes align with their mission, vision, and culture, the likelihood of long-term retention increases significantly.

Hiring the right person stands as the cornerstone of building a cohesive and committed workforce. When employees feel that they make a good fit with the organization, they are more likely to be engaged, motivated, and loyal. This alignment leads to higher job satisfaction and reduces the risk of turnover. In contrast, a poor hiring decision can lead to dissatisfaction, disengagement, and, ultimately, higher turnover rates. Therefore, it remains crucial for organizations to adopt rigorous and effective hiring practices to ensure that they bring onboard individuals who will thrive within their unique environment.

In today's technologically advanced world, numerous tools and technologies assist organizations in improving their hiring processes. These technologies can enhance the accuracy and efficiency of hiring decisions, ensuring a better fit between the candidate and the organization. For instance, advanced applicant tracking systems (ATS) can streamline the recruitment process by efficiently managing candidate information and applications. Artificial intelligence (AI) and machine learning algorithms can analyze vast amounts of data to identify candidates who possess the desired skills and attributes, reducing bias and improving the objectivity of hiring decisions.

Moreover, technologies such as psychometric testing, video interviewing platforms, and predictive analytics can provide deeper insights into a candidate's personality, work style, and cultural fit. These tools enable organizations to assess not only the technical competencies of candidates but also their potential to integrate seamlessly into the organizational culture. By leveraging these technologies, organizations can make more informed and strategic hiring decisions, ultimately enhancing employee retention.

Incorporating a comprehensive onboarding process that reinforces the organization's values and culture from the outset helps new hires acclimate to their new environment, understand their role and responsibilities, and feel welcomed and supported. This initial experience sets the tone for their tenure with the organization and can significantly impact their long-term engagement and retention.

In conclusion, while the strategies discussed throughout this book are crucial for retaining current employees, the journey to effective employee retention begins with hiring the right individuals. Organizations must prioritize recruiting candidates who align with their mission, vision, and values to build a committed and cohesive workforce. Utilizing advanced technologies and adopting comprehensive hiring practices can significantly enhance the accuracy of hiring decisions, ensuring a better fit and ultimately leading to improved retention rates. As we move forward, it is imperative for organizations to recognize the critical role that hiring the right person plays in fostering a stable and engaged workforce.

SUMMARY OF CHAPTER 8: INCREASE THE ODDS

Chapter 8 emphasizes the importance of tailoring strategies to meet the unique values and expectations of Generation Y (Millennials) and Generation Z (Zoomers) employees to improve retention. It highlights the contrasting priorities of these two generations and the need for organizations to create a culture that balances flexibility, innovation, stability, and purpose.

Millennials focus on a workplace culture that aligns with their personal values, emphasizing teamwork, collaboration, and inclusivity. They value job security and structured career advancement, preferring environments where long-term growth opportunities are evident. Activities like team-building and professional development remain key motivators for this generation.

In contrast, Gen Z prioritizes flexibility, diversity, and innovation. They seek immediate job satisfaction and opportunities for meaningful work, valuing mentorship that provides autonomy and fosters creativity. For this generation, flexibility in work schedules and personalized career development paths hold significant weight in their decision to remain with an organization.

The chapter also delves into the role of work-life balance, noting that Millennials prefer structured initiatives that support both personal and professional growth, such as professional development sessions and team-building activities. Meanwhile,

Gen Z values flexibility and autonomy, favoring roles allowing them to manage their time independently, while maintaining a balance between work and personal pursuits.

Career development emerges as a critical factor for both generations, albeit in different forms. Millennials prefer clear career paths and leadership opportunities, while Gen Z seeks diverse experiences, immediate challenges, and roles that allow for innovation and skill-building. Tailored approaches to mentorship, leadership development, and rotational programs can help address these generational needs.

Finally, the chapter underscores that retention starts with hiring the right candidates. Organizations must use advanced technologies such as AI-driven tools, psychometric testing, and comprehensive onboarding processes to ensure alignment between candidates' values and organizational culture. By fostering a collaborative and inclusive environment, companies can create a workforce that feels engaged, challenged, and motivated to stay.

KEY BULLET POINTS

- **Generational Priorities:**
  - *Millennials (Gen Y)*: Value collaboration, inclusivity, and job security.
  - *Gen Z*: Focus on flexibility, innovation, and immediate job satisfaction.

- **Workplace Culture:**
  - Gen Y favors teamwork and structured activities.
  - Gen Z values autonomy, diversity, and corporate social responsibility.

- **Work-Life Balance:**
  - Gen Y: Structured initiatives like team-building and development sessions.

> Gen Z: Flexibility in hours and autonomy over schedules.

- **Career Development:**
  - › Gen Y: Clear paths for long-term growth and leadership roles.
  - › Gen Z: Opportunities for diverse experiences and immediate challenges.

- **Retention Strategies:**
  - › Tailored mentorship and leadership development programs.
  - › Rotational roles and skill-building opportunities.
  - › Flexible work arrangements for both generations.

- **Hiring Practices:**
  - › Use advanced technologies for better candidate alignment.
  - › Comprehensive onboarding to integrate new hires into the culture.

KEY SKILLS AND APPROACHES

- **Cultural Sensitivity:** Understand and adapt to generational differences in workplace values.
- **Mentorship:** Provide tailored mentorship programs that balance guidance with autonomy.
- **Leadership Development:** Offer structured paths for Millennials and innovative challenges for Gen Z.
- **Flexibility:** Implement flexible scheduling and work arrangements.
- **Technology Integration:** Use AI, psychometric testing, and ATS for precise hiring decisions.
- **Work-Life Balance Initiatives:** Develop programs that cater to each generation's needs.

- **Career Pathways:** Design rotational programs and diverse projects for growth.
- **Onboarding Excellence:** Ensure new hires feel supported and aligned with organizational values.

QUESTIONS FOR DEEPER UNDERSTANDING

1. How can organizations balance the differing priorities of Millennials and Gen Z in their workplace culture?
2. What strategies can employers use to address the job security needs of Millennials, while meeting the flexibility demands of Gen Z?
3. How does a company's commitment to corporate social responsibility and inclusivity impact Gen Z retention?
4. What role do advanced hiring technologies play in improving retention from the outset?
5. How can mentorship programs be tailored to offer autonomy for Gen Z, while providing structured guidance for Millennials?
6. What specific work-life balance initiatives could effectively cater to both generations?
7. How does transparency and open communication foster trust and loyalty among Gen Z employees?
8. What steps can organizations take to design career development programs that appeal to both generations?
9. How can companies evaluate their current retention strategies to ensure they align with generational needs?
10. What are the potential risks of failing to address generational differences in retention strategies, and how can they be mitigated?

CITATION:

1. 8 ways Gen Z will change the workforce. (n.d.-b). Stanford University. https://news.stanford.edu/stories/2024/02/8-things -expect-gen-z-coworker

2. Rank, S., & Contreras, F. (2021). Do Millennials pay attention to Corporate Social Responsibility in comparison to previous generations? Are they motivated to lead in times of transformation? A qualitative review of generations, CSR and work motivation. International Journal of Corporate Social Responsibility, 6(1). https://doi.org/10.1186/s40991-020 -00058-y

3. Chamchan, C., & Kittisuksathit, S. (n.d.). Generation Y Employees in Thai Workplaces: What Make Them Stay or Leave. Animo Repository. https://animorepository.dlsu.edu.ph/apssr /vol19/iss1/5/

4. Syahputra, M. J., & Hendarman, A. F. (2024). The Relationship between Key Factors and Gen Z Employee Retention in Indonesian FMCG Start-Ups. International Journal of Current Science Research and Review, 07(07). https://doi.org/10.47191 /ijcsrr/v7-i7-85

5. Masood, R. Z. (2024). Strategies for employee retention in high turnover sectors: An empirical investigation. International Journal of Research in Human Resource Management, 6(1), 33–41. https://doi.org/10.33545/26633213.2024.v6.i1a.167

6. Hassan, M. M., Jambulingam, M., Alagas, E. N., Uzir, M. U. H., & Halbusi, H. A. (2020). Necessities and Ways of Combating Dissatisfactions at Workplaces Against the Job-Hopping

Generation Y Employees. Global Business Review, 24(6), 1276–1301. https://doi.org/10.1177/0972150920926966

7. Bhuiyan, M. M. K., Hassan, M. M., Alam, M. K., Thakur, O. A., & Nasrin, H. (2023). THE IMPACT OF EXTRINSIC MOTIVATION AND WORK-LIFE BALANCE ON GENERATION Y'S CONTENTMENT OF PRIVATE SECTORS IN BANGLADESH. Journal of Nusantara Studies (JONUS), 8(1), 1–25. https://doi.org/10.24200/jonus.vol8iss1pp1-25

CHAPTER 9

CONTINUOUS IMPROVEMENT

THE EXECUTIVE VIEWPOINT

Jeanine Selover
ITS, Vice President of Organizational Development
TOPIC: How Offering Competitive Benefits Packages Improves Employee Retention

Through more than 20 years of experience in roles that are either directly or indirectly involved in recruiting, the landscape of candidates has changed quite a bit, but the fact that benefits are important to getting and retaining good talent has not changed. The way candidates look at the benefits and which ones they see as most important is very different. Years ago, the main benefits candidates wanted to know about were the medical benefits and how well the health benefits work for their families. With new laws allowing many young employees to stay on their parent's medical benefits until age 26, employer-sponsored medical benefits do not hold the same value they once did. The newer generations are focused on different benefits such as work-life balance, company culture, and being part of an organization that aligns with their values.

I think one of the most important parts of offering competitive benefits packages to improve the retention of Gen Y and Z is to listen to what is important to them and align and educate them. What we have found is that a large portion of employees do not even know what all their benefits are. For example, mental health has been a very popular topic in recent years. About more than 90% of companies offer Employee Assistant Programs (EAPs). These programs are designed to provide free and confidential assessments, short-term counseling, and referrals to support growing mental health issues. However, it is estimated that only 4% of employees ever use this benefit, and furthermore, most don't even know it is available to them.

Another common benefit the newer generations are asking for is work-life balance. There is a constant challenge to employers on how to provide flexibility while also running an efficient and successful business. Some companies can give completely flexible schedules for their employees, but for others, it is not an option. For companies that require a more traditional work schedule or in-house work, how else can you support work-life balance? It can take some creativity, but some examples might be providing an in-office gym so employees can work out during their lunch hour versus when they get home in the evening or maybe providing lunch a few days a week so employees do not need to spend so much time meal prepping. Showing employees that you hear them and are coming up with ways to support their needs is the benefit they are looking for and will create their loyalty and improve retention.

As we reach the conclusion of this book on employee retention, we acknowledge that while numerous strategies can significantly enhance an organization's ability to retain employees, no absolute guarantees exist. Human beings remain inherently complex, with needs and desires that evolve over time. This reality makes the task of retaining 100 percent of employees virtually impossible. However, by understanding these complexities and applying the tools and strategies discussed throughout this book, organizations can improve their chances of retaining a larger portion of their workforce.

This book has explored various dimensions of employee retention, from the critical role of leadership and organizational culture to the impact of comprehensive employee benefits and a healthy work environment. We have delved into the specific expectations of Gen Y and Z, highlighting their unique needs and the importance of aligning organizational practices with these expectations. We have also emphasized the foundational significance of hiring the right individuals, whose values and skills align with the organization's mission and culture. Each of these components plays a vital role in creating an environment where employees feel valued, supported, and motivated to stay.

Despite the best efforts and the most effective strategies, the inherent unpredictability of human behavior remains a significant challenge. Employees' personal circumstances, career aspirations, and external opportunities constantly change, influencing their decisions to stay with or leave an organization. Economic shifts, technological advancements, and social changes also play a role in shaping the employment landscape, adding further complexity to retention efforts.

The tools and strategies discussed in this book provide a robust framework for addressing these challenges. Effective leadership, clear communication of core values, and the creation of a positive organizational culture represent fundamental components in fostering a sense of belonging and commitment among employees. Comprehensive employee benefits that address physical, mental, and financial well-being, along with opportunities for professional growth and development, remain critical in meeting the needs of today's workforce. Additionally, ensuring a healthy and supportive work environment where employees feel respected can significantly enhance their engagement and loyalty.

However, organizations must always recognize that employee retention cannot be seen as a one-time effort but an ongoing process. Organizations need continuous assessment and adaptation to respond to the ever-changing needs and expectations of employees. Organizations must remain flexible and innovative, willing to evolve their practices and policies to stay relevant and competitive in attracting and retaining top talent.

Moreover, the importance of open communication and feedback cannot be overstated. Regularly engaging with employees to understand their concerns, aspirations, and suggestions can provide valuable insights into how the organization can better support them. This dialogue fosters a culture of trust where employees feel heard and valued.

As we conclude, we offer some essential thoughts. While no guarantees exist in retaining every employee, utilizing the strategies outlined in this book will undoubtedly enhance an organization's ability to retain more of its workforce. By prioritizing employee well-being, fostering a positive culture, and continuously adapting to meet the evolving needs of employees, organizations can build a resilient and committed workforce.

Ultimately, the journey of employee retention is one of ongoing learning and improvement. Organizations that embrace this journey with a genuine commitment to their employees' success and happiness will find themselves better positioned to navigate the complexities of the modern workforce. While 100 percent retention may remain an elusive goal, the pursuit of creating a supportive, engaging, and fulfilling work environment holds the promise of achieving significant gains in employee loyalty and organizational success.

SUMMARY OF CHAPTER 9: CONTINUOUS IMPROVEMENT

Chapter 9 emphasizes that while employee retention can be significantly enhanced through strategic efforts, achieving 100% retention is unrealistic due to the inherent complexity of human behavior and external influences. However, by applying the strategies outlined in the book, organizations can create environments that increase the likelihood of retaining a greater portion of their workforce.

The chapter recaps the central themes explored in the book, including the vital roles of leadership, organizational culture, comprehensive benefits, professional development, and hiring aligned individuals. These elements collectively foster environments where employees feel valued, supported, and engaged. Tailoring strategies to meet the distinct expectations of Generations Y and Z remains critical, particularly in addressing their priorities for meaningful work, flexibility, inclusivity, and growth.

Despite the best strategies, retention remains influenced by ever-changing factors such as employees' personal circumstances, external opportunities, and societal shifts. This unpredictability highlights the importance of ongoing assessment and adaptation. Employee retention should not be seen as a one-time initiative but as a continuous process requiring flexibility and innovation to address evolving workforce dynamics.

Open communication and feedback loops are pivotal in understanding employee needs and enhancing retention strategies. Engaging with employees to understand their aspirations and concerns fosters trust and provides actionable insights for improving workplace policies and practices. This two-way dialogue creates a culture of belonging and respect, further strengthening employee commitment.

The chapter concludes with a call to action for organizations to embrace continuous improvement as a guiding principle. By remaining committed to fostering positive workplace experiences and prioritizing employee well-being, organizations can build resilient and loyal workforces. While achieving perfect retention is unattainable, the pursuit of creating a supportive and engaging environment offers substantial rewards in employee satisfaction and organizational success.

KEY BULLET POINTS

- **Retention Challenges:**
    - Achieving 100% retention is unrealistic due to the unpredictability of human behavior and external factors.
    - Economic, technological, and social changes influence employee decisions.

- **Core Retention Strategies:**
    - Effective leadership and communication of core values.
    - Positive organizational culture that fosters belonging and purpose.
    - Comprehensive benefits addressing physical, mental, and financial well-being.
    - Opportunities for professional development and growth.
    - Hiring individuals aligned with organizational values and culture.

- **Continuous Improvement:**
  - › Employee retention is an ongoing process requiring assessment, adaptation, and flexibility.
  - › Organizations must innovate and evolve to stay competitive in attracting and retaining talent.

- **Communication and Feedback:**
  - › Regular employee engagement to understand concerns and aspirations.
  - › Open dialogue fosters trust and strengthens organizational commitment.

- **Conclusion:**
  - › Prioritizing well-being and fostering a positive culture enhances retention.
  - › Creating an engaging work environment leads to significant gains in loyalty and organizational success.

KEY SKILLS AND APPROACHES

- **Leadership Excellence:** Develop leadership skills that inspire trust, align with values, and foster a positive culture.
- **Adaptive Strategies:** Build flexibility into policies to respond to changing employee needs and external conditions.
- **Feedback Mechanisms:** Implement regular feedback loops to gain insights into employee satisfaction and concerns.
- **Cultural Alignment:** Focus on hiring practices that ensure alignment with organizational values and mission.
- **Professional Development:** Provide opportunities for career growth and skill-building.
- **Well-Being Initiatives:** Design benefits and programs that address employees' holistic well-being.

- **Innovation:** Continuously innovate workplace practices to stay relevant and competitive.

QUESTIONS FOR DEEPER UNDERSTANDING

1. What specific strategies can organizations use to remain adaptable to evolving workforce expectations?
2. How can organizations create a feedback system that fosters trust and provides actionable insights?
3. What are some innovative approaches to tailoring retention strategies for a multigenerational workforce?
4. In what ways can leadership styles impact the success of retention efforts?
5. How can organizations strike a balance between offering flexibility and maintaining productivity?
6. What role does employee onboarding play in establishing a foundation for retention?
7. How can companies measure the effectiveness of their retention strategies over time?
8. What are the potential risks of not continuously improving employee retention practices?
9. How can small and medium-sized enterprises adopt robust retention strategies with limited resources?
10. What examples of continuous improvement practices have proven effective in organizations facing high turnover rates?

ABOUT THE AUTHORS

DR. JEFF BELSKY

Throughout his 30-year professional career, Dr. Jeff Belsky has worked for several large, well-known organizations in numerous cities and sectors. He held various roles within those organizations, including several C-suite positions. He currently serves as the Director of Strategy and Consultant Development and a Certified Executive Coach for Solutions 21, a global leadership development organization based in Pittsburgh, Pennsylvania. Previously, he was the Vice President of Strategy for an educational organization in Pittsburgh, Pennsylvania. Jeff also has been an adjunct business professor for 25 years teaching at five universities, two of which are internationally based.

A talented facilitator and speaker, Jeff has trained and consulted with several prominent corporations nationwide. He also has personally coached more than 400 individuals from all business sectors, authored several articles and a book, "*The*

Leadership Toolboxes," and has dedicated his time to improving organizational leadership.

Jeff received his undergraduate degree in marketing, MBA, and doctorate in business administration (DBA) from Liberty University. He resides in Florida and has been married for nearly 40 years to Johnene, his high school sweetheart. He has three lovely children—Jordan, Michaela, and Aaron, and two golden retrievers. He enjoys traveling, hiking, great food, and anything pertaining to his family.

TOM SHANDY

Tom Shandy has 25 years of combined leadership experience in business and as a military officer and U.S. Army Ranger. After receiving his undergraduate degree from Middle Tennessee State University, he began a tenure as a program director for a successful small business chain training managers and supervisors, which resulted in dynamic organizational growth. Tom later joined the U.S. Army and became an Infantry Officer, leading soldiers during combat operations in Iraq and Afghanistan. He later taught leadership and planning skills at the U.S. Army Ranger School. During his military career, he received additional advanced degrees in Adult Learning and Leadership from Kansas State University, Operational Art and Design Thinking from the School for Advanced Military Studies (SAMS), and Command and General Staff College certifications.

A facilitator and speaker, Tom currently serves as the Director of Organizational Development and certified coach for Solutions 21, a global leader development firm based in Pittsburgh, Pennsylvania. At Solutions 21, he has coached and mentored hundreds of business leaders at all levels in business strategy, problem-solving, and overall employee retention through dynamic leadership.

Tom currently resides in Dahlonega, Georgia, with his wife of 20 years and two daughters. He enjoys being involved with the community and volunteers with local non-profit organizations.